# HOW TO BUILD A SMALL GROUPS MINISTRY

## NEAL F. McBRIDE

NAVPRESS

BRINGING TRUTH TO LIFE

P.O. BOX 35001, COLORADO SPRINGS, COLORADO 80935

The Navigators is an international Christian organization. Jesus Christ gave His followers the Great Commission to go and make disciples (Matthew 28:19). The aim of The Navigators is to help fulfill that commission by multiplying laborers for Christ in every nation.

ISBN 08910-97694

Some of the anecdotal illustrations in this book are true to life and are included with the permission of the persons involved. All other illustrations are composites of real situations, and any resemblance to people living or dead is coincidental.

Unless otherwise identified, all Scripture quotations in this publication are taken from the *New American Standard Bible* (NASB), © The Lockman Foundation 1960, 1962, 1963, 1968, 1971, 1972, 1973, 1975, 1977. Another version used is the *HOLY BIBLE: NEW INTER- NATIONAL VERSION*® (NIV®), Copyright © 1973, 1978, 1984 by International Bible Society, used by permission of Zondervan Publishing House, all rights reserved.

Printed in the United States of America

3 4 5 6 7 8 9 10 11 12 13 14 15 / 99 98 97 96 95

# CONTENTS

90554

*To Lyman Coleman,*
*founder and president, Serendipity House,*
*visionary small-groups spokesperson,*
*brother in Christ and friend,*
*a true eccentric and fun-loving guy*

# ACKNOWLEDGMENTS

This book reflects my many years in small-group ministries, but numerous unnamed people contributed to my groups education, so their thoughts and ideas are also reflected in this book. Thanks everyone!

The Old Testament book of Ecclesiastes tells us repeatedly that there is "nothing new under the sun." Such is the case with small-group ministries. Any ideas or thoughts borrowed without giving due credit was unintentional.

A special thank-you goes to my wife and children—Reva, Kyle, and Katie—for encouraging me to put my thoughts and experience in writing. Likewise, a big thank-you goes to everyone who has endured being in a group with me over the years.

# HOW TO USE
# THIS HANDBOOK

This planning guide is designed for lay leaders, pastors, professional staff members, and anyone else interested in small-group ministries within their local church. Churches vary in size, location, affiliation, and personality, but the general techniques used in organizing and administering small-group ministries are useful in nearly all situations. With this in mind, this handbook recognizes that good planning is one key to successful small groups. Simply put, effective planning lays the foundation for effective groups.

Some basic concepts about organizing and administering a small-groups ministry are presented in twelve logical steps. In reality, however, the suggested steps do not always occur in the exact order presented. Organizing and administering any program is a continual process of asking and reasking questions, redefining goals and objectives, devising creative alternatives, adjusting to changing circumstances, and incorporating new resources. The steps outlined for you here can and must be adapted to your needs. Feel free to adjust the steps in any manner you see fit.

Some people find the suggested steps easy to accomplish, but others struggle with them. Every method or step doesn't work exactly the same for every person. Try each step for yourself to see if it's right for your situation. When you've finished the manual you'll be familiar with a variety of organization and administration options. This will allow you to think of new methods specific to your own set of circumstances.

This handbook is a basic primer that includes three essential parts:

1. A case-study example
2. Presentation of the twelve steps
3. Worksheets for developing your own plan

This book is designed as a *workbook*, so blank worksheets are provided for you to develop your own plan. (Limited permission is given to copy these worksheets for use in conjunction with your study of *How to Build a Small-Groups Ministry*. No pages in any other part of this book may be copied, nor may the worksheets be copied for any reason other than actual use with this book.)

To help in the planning process, a case study serves as the "subject" used in the sample worksheets. The case study involves a fictional lay leader's hypothetical experiences—Mr. Don Swan, an elder in a church ministering to about 325 regular adult attenders. His goal is to plan a small-groups ministry. This middle-of-the-road example is applicable to churches of any size. Don't forget, you are free to add, subtract, and modify steps to fit your situation.

Before starting your journey through this handbook, please do the following:

1. Pray—practice the biblical command to *pray without ceasing* (1 Thessalonians 5:17).
2. Quickly read all the way through this manual to get a feel for the whole planning process.
3. Review *How to Lead Small Groups* (NavPress, 1990) to familiarize yourself with the biblical basis for small groups and the dynamics involved in leading one small group. After all, a successful small-groups ministry is based on many successful small groups.
4. Plan to complete all the planning steps in this manual *before* you start implementing your specific small-groups-ministry strategy.
5. Enlist others to help you. Remember, among the first things Jesus Christ did when He began His earthly ministry was to put together His team—the apostles.

Building an effective small-groups ministry is an orderly, analytical process—at times this will run contrary to the casual way many churches operate. The grind of day-to-day crisis management often omits careful planning. Don't lose hope. The process described in this book is more than a means to cope. It can help you develop a systematic method for planning many other ministries within your church.

To borrow an old advertising slogan from Nike, the athletic-shoe manufacturer, *Just Do It!* No one is perfect. Sure, you'll make some mistakes. Just remind yourself, the only poor small-groups-ministry plan is . . . no plan at all. Now, repeat after me: *I can do all things through Him (Christ) who strengthens me* (Philippians 4:13).

---

*Please note:* The twelve steps presented in this handbook represent a *generic* approach to planning a small-groups ministry. Therefore, please tailor the steps and suggested procedures to fit your specific situation.

*There's no one right way to develop a groups ministry.* So, don't be afraid to experiment. It's okay to change your mind if you discover a method doesn't work or if you find a better way to do something.

# A CASE STUDY

**Meet Main Street Church**

Main Street Church is a typical congregation located in Niceville, USA. With a population of 24,566 citizens, Niceville is on the main highway and serves as a bedroom community for Gotham City, nine miles away. The community is home for Bates Electronics, the state's largest employer. Here are Main Street Church's vital statistics:

*Founded: 1950*

*Affiliation*
Mainstream Evangelical Denomination of America

*Governance*
Board of Elders—fourteen active members; each chairs a specific ministry team (committee); Mr. Don Swan chairs the Small-Groups-Ministry Team.

*Pastoral Staff*
   PASTOR—Patrick Oden; seminary graduate; forty-two years old, married to Jane, two teenage children; just completed his third year at the church, twelfth year in the ministry; served in two previous churches.
   YOUTH PASTOR—Ray Gleason; Bible college graduate; twenty-seven years old, married to Elizabeth, one baby son; began his ministry eight months ago; third church ministry out of Bible college.

*Membership*
326 adult members; a diverse membership with various socioeconomic backgrounds; about 24 percent of the adult members work for Bates Electronics, 33 percent commute to their jobs in Gotham City, and the remainder work in the community or are retired. No one age group dominates, but forty-three is the average age for adult members.

*Worship Attendance*
325 adults on an average morning, while an average of 54 people attend the evening service.

*Sunday School*
On average, 183 people attend; including three adult classes with a total average of 66 adults.

*Facilities*
Older facilities, but their size and condition are adequate. There is a growing interest in remodeling and perhaps adding a gym.

*History*
Pastor Oden is only the third minister to serve the church. He began his ministry just two months after the second minister, Pastor Taylor, who was there only sixteen months, departed under difficult circumstances. The founding minister, Pastor Bishop, retired. There was a two-year gap between Pastor Bishop's leaving and Pastor Taylor's arrival. Pastor

Bishop was very well liked and admired. The search committee was unsuccessful in its attempts to find someone just like him and settled on Pastor Taylor after three other candidates turned down the job.

An excellent scholar and a fair preacher, Pastor Taylor spent the majority of his time studying and preparing sermons. Unlike Pastor Bishop, he did little visitation and was vocal in his dislike for counseling or "hand-holding," as he called it.

Membership peaked at 535 just before Pastor Bishop's retirement. Most church members missed his grandfatherly image and warmth. Pastor Taylor was perceived as cold, aloof, and uncaring. Members soon began to leave. Alarmed at losing members, the Board of Elders met in private and decided to ask for his resignation. He resisted and called for a church vote. By constitution, a two-thirds vote was required to remove him from office; it failed by three votes. He felt it was God's will for him to stay. Six weeks later he announced his resignation. He was going to pursue a Ph.D. in communications at State University.

The membership count was down to 286 on Pastor Oden's first Sunday.

Pastor Oden had a difficult first year at the church. He was often unfavorably compared with both of his predecessors. His sermons didn't have as much content as Pastor Taylor's, and he wasn't as warm as Pastor Bishop. It was a difficult experience.

Undaunted, but battling discouragement, Pastor Oden pressed on. Many hours were spent in prayer and discussing the situation with two wise, long-serving church leaders. He worked hard getting to know his people and building relationships. In addition, some creative changes brought healthy increases in the average attendance at the morning worship service.

The church is recovering from its slump. New families began joining the church within the past eighteen months. As a result, Ray Gleason was called to serve as their first youth pastor. The future looks encouraging.

Both pastors and all the elected church leaders are excited over God's apparent blessings. They are also convinced that Main Street Church cannot rest on its present success. New ideas and ministries are needed.

Recently one of the elders, Mr. Swan, approached Pastor Oden. What about small groups? Mr. Swan joined the elder board six months before Pastor Bishop retired. Originally he accepted the responsibility for putting together a committee to explore small-group possibilities. But with Pastor Bishop's retirement and Pastor Taylor's dislike of groups, Mr. Swan gave up on small groups and assumed leadership for missions and evangelism.

Mr. Swan's interest in small groups hadn't died, however. Several weeks ago he attended a one-day small-groups seminar sponsored by Serendipity (see below). The next day he made an appointment with his pastor. Pastor Oden welcomed the idea but was too busy to undertake yet another area of responsibility. Would Mr. Swan consider chairing a small-groups-ministry team? After discussing the idea with his wife, who agreed to join him in the effort, Mr. Swan eagerly accepted.

The planning example provided in this handbook is based on Main Street Church's experience. Main Street Church doesn't really exist; it represents many churches the author has worked with over the past twenty-five years. Serendipity, however, does exist. It is a small-groups ministry founded and directed by Lyman Colemen. For information, write to:

Serendipity
P.O. Box 1012
Littleton, CO 80160

STEP ONE

# PLANNING
# TO PLAN

*The plans of the diligent lead surely to advantage,*
*But everyone who is hasty comes surely to poverty.*
PROVERBS 21:5

**OVERVIEW**—The purpose of this chapter is to assist you in:

1. Identifying the key persons who will help you plan and implement your groups ministry.

2. Determining the planning goals for your groups ministry.

3. Clarifying your planning boundaries.

**P**lanning requires planning. That's right! Developing a realistic small-groups ministry demands that you organize and prepare your planning process. Preplanning provides the necessary guidance you need to conduct the actual groups planning process. Investing time and energy in preplanning is vital. *Please* don't overlook this foundational, essential step.

Step 1 and step 2 are linked together. In actuality, step 2 is a substep within step 1. But because step 2 deals with such an important issue—authority—it warrants being a separate, distinct step. Most people find it helpful to consider steps 1 and 2 at the same time.

Planning to plan, or preplanning, is aimed at *identifying, securing,* and *coordinating* the *resources* and *conditions* necessary to do the actual planning needed in putting together a workable small-groups ministry. Starting with *resources* and *conditions*, let's clarify our terms:

*RESOURCES* are the tangible, available means to accomplish the task. There are three basic categories: people, time, and finances. In other words, the *people* and *"things"* you need to get the planning job done. Be realistic. There are limitations to the resources at your disposal; know what they are and stay within bounds.

*CONDITIONS* are the spiritual, emotional, and experiential circumstances that surround the planning process—the atmosphere and attitudes you must promote that are necessary for successful planning in general and small groups in particular.

*IDENTIFYING* means to recognize and select the resources needed to accomplish the task and to determine what resources are necessary. Identifying the resources you'll need is at the heart of the planning process. But remember, be realistic.

*SECURING* means to obtain the identified, necessary resources and then to guard against the loss or misuse of those resources. When compared with the identification process, acquiring the needed resources is usually more difficult. What you need and what you get may differ, and it usually does. Be prepared to improvise and/or readjust your needs in light of the limitations you're likely to encounter.

Every situation is different from each other, yet every situation has similarities. Consequently, there are some preplanning areas you need to think about from your unique context and set of circumstances. The following categories represent key issues, resources, and conditions that set the stage for your actual planning process. Feel free to add or subtract issues if you find it necessary.

## KNOW WHERE YOU STAND

Who are you? Who you are—your position within the church leadership or hierarchy—is an important consideration. The planning dynamics change depending on whether you're *the* pastor; a member of the pastoral staff; an elder (deacon, trustee, overseer, etc.); or a motivated member of the congregation (a layperson). Ideally, these positional distinctions shouldn't make any difference, but unfortunately they do. So you must know where you stand and act accordingly.

Reality dictates that the more authority—the ability to make final decisions—you have, the more likely and quickly you'll succeed in effecting change. It's usually easier, but not always, for pastors to introduce and implement programmatic changes; people expect pastors to suggest new ideas. On the other hand, if you're a motivated layperson without any recognized leadership role, don't despair—success is still within your reach. Just be prepared for a longer and a bit more difficult process. This means that before you can even attempt to share ("sell") the vision for small groups, you must gain a hearing. Doing so may prove easy or difficult, depending on your situation.

If you're an elected or appointed lay leader in your church, you fit somewhere in between pastors and motivated laypersons. The amount of authority invested in your leadership role places you nearer or farther away from the pastor's ability to sell, plan, introduce, and implement a small-groups ministry.

What's the bottom line? Simply know and accept your role and position within your church's decisionmaking hierarchy. If necessary, be prepared to spend whatever time it takes to enhance your credibility as a groups ministry spokesperson.

## THE PLANNING TEAM

You'll need help in planning. It takes a team. Programs planned by one person are usually less successful than those planned by a collaborative team effort. The old adage "Two (three, four, five, etc.) heads are better than one" *is true!* Consequently, the most important preplanning step is to identify and enlist others to help you plan and implement the groups ministry.

Later in the planning process you'll need to consider personnel matters related to implementing and running a groups ministry. But right now, it's crucial for you to invest adequate time in selecting and enlisting the right people to assist you by serving on your planning team.

### The Planning Team: Selection

Putting together the planning team (committee, commission, board, task force, etc.) is perhaps the most important thing you'll do at this point in your small-groups ministry. Guided by the Holy Spirit, pick the members carefully. *Experience has proven that the team's membership is the single most critical factor in assuring a group ministry's initial success.* These people not only set the ministry's organizational structure, but more importantly, they become the key spokespersons for sharing the vision with other church members.

There is no "right" team size. Nevertheless, the chart below outlines some suggestions for team size based on the number of adults who participate in your church (members and nonmembers). You aren't obligated to comply with the chart standards. Just remember, the more people involved—within reason—the more individuals you'll have to plan and support the groups ministry.

| GUIDELINES FOR PLANNING TEAM SIZE | |
|---|---|
| **Church Size** (Average Adult Participants) | **Team Size** (Number of Members) |
| 50 to 150 | 3 |
| 151 to 500 | 3 to 5 |
| 501 to 1,000 | 5 to 7 |
| 1,001 to 1,500 | 7 to 9 |
| 1,501 to 2,000 | 9 to 11 |
| 2,000 or more | 11 to 13 |

Once you determine how many people you want on the planning team, continue to saturate the selection process with time and prayer. Avoid speeding up or slowing down; only you can determine the correct pace. Pray and ask God to show you which people to approach, relying on the Holy Spirit to guide you to the right individuals. It's difficult to explain exactly what it means to rely on the Holy Spirit for guidance in the selection process; however, listed below are some suggestions that may help you discern God's will.

## SELECTING A PLANNING TEAM

1. *Develop a prospect list.* List people you think might have interest and skills in group ministries. Another good source for potential team members is to ask for suggestions from your pastor and other people you trust. Look for individuals who meet the qualifications for church membership (or leadership if you have no formal membership) and have the time to invest in a groups ministry. Experience with groups is very useful, but not an absolute necessity. "Natural" leadership ability isn't as important as the person's willingness to serve and learn.

If you're not the pastor, on the pastoral team, or a member of your church's governing board, it's a good idea to include one or more of these individuals on the planning team. It's important because such an individual gives you a direct link to the top leadership in your church.

2. *Pray over your prospect list.* Ask God to give you the opportunity to present the ministry challenge to those persons He wants involved.

3. *Develop a brief, general job description* that outlines the team's task and responsibilities. You may tailor the following example to your needs:

---

### JOB DESCRIPTION
#### Small-Groups Ministry Planning Team

**Task**
- Serve on the planning team to design and implement a small-groups ministry in our church.

**Responsibilities**
- Contribute the time, energy, and ideas necessary to assist in planning a groups ministry.
- Attend all planning sessions.
- Accept and accomplish specific subtasks related to planning and implementing the groups ministry.
- Help promote the small-groups ministry.
- Pray for wisdom, for yourself and the team as a whole.

**Qualifications**
- Excited about the vision for small groups in our church.
- A church member (or regular attender).
- Committed to being a team player.
- Ideally, prior experience with group ministries.
- Willing to serve until the groups ministry is implemented.

**Resources**
- A small, but adequate budget.
- Necessary clerical assistance.
- Continuing support for our pastor.
- All expenses paid to attend the Heartlands Small-Groups Conference.

---

4. *Seek the opportunity to have a private conversation with each prospect.* Lay out the ministry vision and opportunity, review the job description, answer questions, and explain why you are asking the person to participate.

5. *Allow the individual enough time to think and pray.* Asking for a decision the first time you introduce the person to the ministry isn't necessary. Follow up in a week or so to get the person's answer.

6. *Avoid twisting arms.* Subtle, coercive efforts to get a person to say yes aren't recommended. In my opinion, if a prospect expresses doubt or a lack of interest, I politely move on. God has someone else in mind.

7. *Aim at the ideal team membership size*, but adjust upward or downward as necessary. Filling all the proposed slots isn't as important as finding the right people.

Generally speaking, identifying and offering the ministry opportunity to preselected individuals is far better than making a general announcement asking for volunteers. Jesus called (recruited) specific individuals to serve as apostles. In my opinion, having a small planning team, one that includes individuals committed to a small-groups ministry, is far better than a larger team involving noncommitted members.

## The Planning Team: Organization

The planning team, like all organizations, needs an organizational structure to function smoothly. Start with as few "positions" as possible. Keep it simple. If later you find there's a need for additional tasks, functions, or jobs, create the necessary organizational position at that point. Stay flexible. Following are some planning suggestions for teams of various sizes. As always, tailor it to your situation and needs.

### Planning Teams with Three to Seven Members

- *Chair*—The team leader; responsible to coordinate all team meetings and activities; represents the team to "higher church authorities."
- *Scribe* (secretary/treasurer)—Keeps team minutes and records; oversees the budget.
- *Recruiting and Training*—Implements the recruiting and training plan devised by the team.

The remaining members assist wherever needed and/or undertake necessary, specific tasks that may arise.

### Planning Teams with Eight or More Members

- *Chair*—Same as previously described.
- *Scribe*—Same as previously described.
- *Recruiting*—Oversees and implements the recruiting plan developed by the team.
- *Training*—Oversees and implements the training plan formulated by the team.
- *Publicity*—Oversees and implements the promotion and publicity plan devised by the team.

Note that the recruiting and leadership-training functions are separate responsibilities. The remaining members assist wherever needed and/or undertake necessary, specific tasks that may arise.

Filling the organizational positions on the planning team can take place at several points along the way: (1) as you recruit prospective planning team members—ask specific individuals you think can do the job to serve on the team and accept a specific role; (2) at the team's first (or second) official meeting; or (3) whenever it's feasible and convenient. Remember, the reason for the organizational structure is to help the team function well. The system must not force the team into rigid patterns or procedures.

### The Planning Team: Operation

Once the team is formed, it's time to begin operating. Find a convenient date, time, and place (somewhere quiet) to hold your first meeting. Be sure to allow at least two hours. Your initial meetings set the tone for the future, so proceed with prudence.

You'd be wise to call or mail each member a reminder of the meeting date, time, and place—in fact, it's a good idea to do this each time you meet. Include a copy of the agenda. Here's an ideal agenda to guide your initial meeting (tailor it to meet your specific needs):

1. Opening prayer.
2. Introductions (if needed).
3. Review the small-groups ministry need and vision for your church.

4. Explain what is involved in planning a groups ministry (briefly explain the twelve steps outlined in this handbook).
5. Discuss team organization and determine who is going to fill the needed positions (you may want to wait until your second meeting).
6. Set a tentative schedule for future meetings.
7. Divide into pairs and pray for your planning team.

For the first six months it's wise to schedule regular meetings. "How often?" you ask. Frequency depends on your situation. You may start out meeting weekly if you're on a short time line, or at least twice per month. Regardless of how often you meet, make certain that your subsequent meetings are productive.

Here's an idea you might find useful at all your meetings. Before adjourning, (1) review any decisions made, (2) summarize what must be done before the next meeting, and (3) clarify who is responsible to accomplish the identified tasks.

## PREPLANNING ISSUES
During its first two or three meetings, the planning team needs to identify, secure, and coordinate the following preplanning issues that affect how the team operates: planning boundaries, planning goals, a basic strategy, and a decision to proceed.

### Planning Boundaries
The sky isn't the limit in most cases. You have certain limitations, boundaries you must work within as you plan the groups ministry. Every church or Christian organization has its particular methods and ways of functioning. To avoid running afoul of the "system," the planning team must know its functional boundaries.

The word *boundary* means different things to different people. I use the word to mean the logical and financial limits you must respect as you plan. Boundaries in this case are not necessarily negative; they're merely the lines on the playing field. Spending a little time up front to identify your boundaries may save you a lot of headaches later.

Listed below are three basic boundaries you must identify and define, plus an "other" category:

AUTHORITY—Authority is the power to make decisions, a very important consideration. How much authority does the planning team possess? Step 2 (page 23) is designed to assist you in examining this issue in depth.

TIME—How much time do you have to plan? An answer to this rudimentary question has at least two different tracks. First, when to begin the planning process, and second, how much time it will take.

You already may be at the planning stage, or perhaps you're just beginning to explore the possibility. Getting started requires a decision (see "The Decision to Proceed" on page 18 for this step) on when to start the formal planning process. An answer depends on the dynamics associated with your situation. You may have the ability to decide for yourself and begin. In contrast, your church may require you to go through a detailed process aimed at evaluating the idea and securing the necessary permission to begin. Whatever the case, be sure to identify and comply with this first time boundary.

Your second time boundary is found in the question, How much time does the planning process take? A simple answer is found in another question: How much time do you have? You may find yourself in the situation where your pastor is asking you to put together a small-groups ministry in just a few short months, or even more difficult, within several weeks. Furthermore, time allotted to planning also varies with church size and level of application. A small-groups ministry for a large church takes more time to plan than it does for a groups ministry within one adult Sunday school class.

Most churches find between six months and one year to be adequate to plan a comprehensive small-groups ministry. However, there isn't a fixed amount of time required to plan. Avoid going too fast or too slow. Keep the planning pace moving, but don't rush ahead unprepared.

*MONEY*—What is your budget? Money is an essential ingredient in all ministries, including small groups. You must find out how much money you have to work with.

When you ask your pastor or church treasurer about a budget, don't be surprised if he or she replies, "How much do you need?" Good question. You may not have a ready answer. After all, at this point you may not know what you need or what you're planning to do. But don't despair, you really don't need a budget to plan. Any planning costs are usually insignificant. However, part of the planning process is to develop a ministry budget (see step 7, page 95). This budgeting process should result in a proposed budget based on what you hope to accomplish. Running the actual groups ministry takes money. A good budget plan, therefore, is required. And keep in mind, the larger the groups ministry, the greater the ongoing costs.

Just a quick word of caution. Even though you don't really need a budget in order to plan your groups ministry and its associated budget, you're wise to ask for some general guidelines—financial boundaries—to stay within as you plan. What financial resources do you have at your disposal to support the planning process? Second, is there an approximate target figure you should seek to stay within as you develop your groups ministry budget?

*OTHER*—Before moving on, ask yourself, "Is there anything else? Are there other boundaries I and the planning team must stay within?" The worksheet at the end of this chapter will help you answer that question.

## Planning Goals

If you aim at nothing, you'll surely hit it. Since hitting nothing isn't your desire, the first thing the planning team *must* do is establish their planning goals. Planning goals are what you want to accomplish during and as a result of planning.

A wide variety of goals are possible, depending on your situation. Later, in step 4, you'll learn more about specific goals and objectives to guide your groups ministry. But at this step all that's needed is to clarify what you hope to accomplish within the planning process, in the broadest terms. Here are some suggested areas around which you can develop your planning goals, but these represent only a few possibilities:

- *Time*—When will the planning process be completed? When will each of the twelve steps be completed? When do you plan to start your first group?
- *Personnel*—What type and how many leaders do you need?
- *Recruiting*—How many leaders will you recruit and by when?
- *Training*—What training will you offer and when will it be held?
- *Publicity*—How much publicity and what type and when?

**The Basic Strategy**

As you plan to plan it's helpful to know where you're headed. So, while it's not a specific preplanning requirement, here are the major tasks—reflecting the twelve steps presented in this handbook—you must complete as you plan your small-groups ministry:

1. Put together your planning team.
2. Develop your small-groups-ministry plan.
3. Secure approval for the plan and permission to proceed.
4. Recruit and train the initial leaders.
5. Implement the groups ministry.

**The Decision to Proceed**

Talking, thinking, and praying about small groups and the related planning process is fine, but at some point the actual process must begin. In some situations this transition is simple—you just decide to start and then proceed. In other cases you may have to go through an elaborate process to have the small-groups-ministry idea approved and receive permission to proceed.

The decision to proceed sets the whole planning process into motion. So, whatever it takes to decide to start the planning process, now is the time to secure that decision. What must the planning team do to secure the necessary permission, if needed, to commence planning? If permission is required, what person or group grants this permission? When is this decision made? These questions will be answered as we proceed through this book.

# STEP ONE WORKSHEET: PLANNING TO PLAN

Church Name: __MAIN STREET CHURCH__    Date: __FEB 6__

1-1. *The person filling out this worksheet and position in the church:*

   Name: __DON SWAN__    Position: __ELDER—SMALL GROUPS__

1-2. *Desired planning team size:* __5__ Members

1-3. *Planning team prospects:*

| Names | Phone | Date Interviewed | Answer |
|---|---|---|---|
| JANE ISLEY | 555-1631 | FEB 15 | NO |
| LU WANG TING | 555-1687 | MAR 8 | NO |
| GRACE ADAMS | 555-4142 | MAR 10 | YES |
| KATHY LARSON | 555-3809 | MAR 13 | NO |
| JEFF EDGAR | 555-2116 | FEB 29 | YES |
| MARY GARCIA | 555-2199 | MAR 6 | NO |
| RON RUSHING | 555-2183 | FEB 15 | NO |
| DEB HOWE | 555-1414 | FEB 19 | YES |
| ELAINE SWAN | 555-1002 | FEB 23 | YES |
| J. D. BURKHOLDER | 555-1608 | FEB 26 | NO |

1-4. *Organizational Structure.* Given the planning team's ideal size, check the needed positions:

☒ Chair      ☒ Scribe      ☐ Recruiting
☒ Recruiting and Training      ☒ Publicity      ☐ Training
☒ Other (specify): RESOURCES (CURRICULUM, ETC.)

1-5. Planning team's first meeting:

   Date: __APR 10__    Time: __7:00 PM__    Place: __SWAN'S HOME__

   Agenda: 1-PRAYER          5-TEAM ORGANIZATION
             2-INTRODUCTIONS     6-FUTURE MEETINGS
             3-SMALL-GROUP VISION    7-DESSERT
             4-OUR MUTUAL TASK

1-6. *Planning boundaries the team must observe:*

Authority (Complete "Step Two Worksheet"): OK . . . SEE STEP 2

Time: START GROUPS WEEK OF SEPT 18—14 WEEKS TO PLAN, RECRUIT, TRAIN LEADERS

Money: LIMITED, BUT CAN DO SOME PUBLICITY—CHECK WITH CHURCH TREASURER

Other: NO GROUPS ON SUNDAY EVENINGS—ELDERS WILL RECONSIDER THIS GUIDELINE IN ONE YEAR

1-7. *The team's planning goals:*
—START 4-6 GROUPS (?) BY THE MIDDLE OF SEPT.
—RECRUIT AND TRAIN 4-8 GROUP LEADERS (OR COUPLES)
—ORGANIZE THE SMALL-GROUPS MINISTRY TEAM TO CARRY ON AFTER THE PLANNING TEAMS JOB IS FINISHED

1-8. *Final planning team roster:*

| | Name | Phone | Position/Office |
|---|---|---|---|
| 1. | DON SWAN | 555-1002 | CHAIR |
| 2. | ELAINE SWAN | 555-1002 | SCRIBE |
| 3. | GRACE ADAMS | 555-4142 | PUBLICITY |
| 4. | JEFF EDGAR | 555-2116 | RESOURCES |
| 5. | DEB HOWE | 555-1414 | RECRUITING |
| 6. | | | AND TRAINING |
| 7. | | | |
| 8. | | | |
| 9. | | | |
| 10. | | | |
| 11. | | | |
| 12. | | | |

*PLANNING TEAM WILL MEET EVERY OTHER SUNDAY IN THE BOARD ROOM—5 TO 6 P.M. (BEFORE THE EVENING SERVICE)

# STEP ONE WORKSHEET: PLANNING TO PLAN

Church Name: _____ Date: _____

1-1. *The person filling out this worksheet and position in the church:*

   Name: _____ Position: _____

1-2. *Desired planning team size:* _____ Members

1-3. *Planning team prospects:*

| Names | Phone | Date Interviewed | Answer |
|-------|-------|------------------|--------|
|       |       |                  |        |

1-4. *Organizational Structure.* Given the planning team's ideal size, check the needed positions:

☐ Chair        ☐ Scribe        ☐ Recruiting
☐ Recruiting and Training        ☐ Publicity        ☐ Training
☐ Other (specify):

1-5. Planning team's first meeting:

   Date: _____ Time: _____ Place: _____

   Agenda:

1-6. *Planning boundaries the team must observe:*

Authority (Complete "Step Two Worksheet"):

Time:

Money:

Other:

1-7. *The team's planning goals:*

1-8. *Final planning team roster:*

| Name | Phone | Position/Office |
| --- | --- | --- |
| 1. _____ | _____ | _____ |
| 2. _____ | _____ | _____ |
| 3. _____ | _____ | _____ |
| 4. _____ | _____ | _____ |
| 5. _____ | _____ | _____ |
| 6. _____ | _____ | _____ |
| 7. _____ | _____ | _____ |
| 8. _____ | _____ | _____ |
| 9. _____ | _____ | _____ |
| 10. _____ | _____ | _____ |
| 11. _____ | _____ | _____ |
| 12. _____ | _____ | _____ |

STEP TWO

# CLARIFYING AUTHORITY

*Many are the plans in a man's heart,*
*But the counsel of the LORD, it will stand.*
PROVERBS 19:21

> **OVERVIEW**—This step is designed to assist you in:
>
> 1. Determining what authority your planning team needs and possesses.
>
> 2. Securing answers to three authority questions.
>
> 3. Identifying your contact person.

**B**efore getting into the actual planning process, there's one more preplanning item that needs your attention. As referred to in step 1, step 2 is a short preplanning step designed to help you clarify some specific authority (power or control) issues within your church as they relate to your small-groups-ministry planning team.

## AUTHORITY

What authority, if any, does your planning team possess to plan and start a small-groups ministry? Likewise, what authority, if any, will future leaders have in overseeing the ongoing small-groups ministry?

Before you can realistically answer the above questions, it's important to define "authority":

*Authority* is the right or authorization to decide and implement decisions; delegated right or power to act.

Two ideas expressed in this definition need further examination. First, authority is essentially power, the power to decide and act. Within every church there are groups and individuals who have power, the authority to make decisions and take action. Second, authority in the church is frequently delegated power. The pastor and/or official governing board entrust other individuals, committees, etc., with the power to plan and lead various ministries within the church. Consequently, knowing what authority you possess—and its source—makes the task of planning and implementing a small-groups ministry much easier.

Power and delegated authority are intimately related. The more power you're given to make decisions and take action on your own, the more authority you possess. This fact is also true for your planning team.

The team's power to make independent, self-directed decisions is directly related to the amount of control the leadership in your church wants to delegate or retain. Control is applied power, the ability to control situations, decisions, actions, etc. It's common for strong (autocratic) pastors to retain all control; simply put, they make all major decisions within their churches. In other churches the power is shared among the pastoral staff and the appropriate governing board or boards (elders, deacons, etc.). In a few rare cases, the governing board holds all the power to control. Who's in control at your church? Who has the power?

With a definition and some introductory comments out of the way, now it's time to answer the question: What authority, if any, does your planning team possess as they plan and start a small-groups ministry?

## AUTHORITY LEVELS

Usually one of the three levels described below characterizes the amount of authority possessed by you and your small-groups-ministry planning team:

*LEVEL ONE—NO AUTHORITY.* The pastor, pastoral staff, or governing board retains all the power to make decisions. The planning team must seek and secure approval for all major and minor decisions related to the groups ministry.

*LEVEL TWO—SOME AUTHORITY.* The pastor, pastoral staff, or governing board delegates some power to make decisions. The planning team must seek and secure approval for selected major decisions but has the authority to implement routine decisions affecting the groups ministry.

*LEVEL THREE—ALL AUTHORITY.* The pastor, pastoral staff, or governing board delegates (or abdicates) all power for making decisions. The planning team is free to do as they please without checking with anyone.

The most common of these is level two, *some authority.* Some decisions are retained by the pastor and/or governing board and some are delegated to the planning team. The key is to find out which decisions, or what type of decisions, are made by whom.

## DECISIONMAKING

When it comes to authority it all boils down to decisionmaking—who makes the decisions? Specifically, who determines how the groups ministry fits into your church? Or more generally, who makes the decisions about your groups ministry—the philosophical and functional decisions?

*PHILOSOPHICAL/THEORETICAL DECISIONS.* Decisions dealing with the nature of and purpose for the small-groups ministry. For example:

- Should we have a small-groups ministry?
- What should a small-group ministry in our church seek to accomplish?
- How will small groups fit into our church programming?
- Can non-church members serve as group leaders?

*FUNCTIONAL/APPLICATION DECISIONS.* Stemming from the philosophical decisions, functional decisions focus on implementing the groups ministry. Step 7, "Nailing Down Organizational

Specifics," provides good examples of the pragmatic decisions you're facing. For example, what types of groups are needed, and what are the groups going to do when they meet?

Within groups ministry, three different levels of decisionmaking are possible: "top" leaders, ministry leaders (first the planning team and then later, the ongoing group-ministry team), and individual group leaders as well as their group members. The ideal situation is to allow each level to make certain appropriate decisions. But here's the rub: What's an "appropriate decision"?

It's helpful to sort out decisionmaking authority—applied authority—among the players in small-group ministries. Assuming a "shared" authority and supervision model, here are some flexible guidelines on who makes what decisions. (You will have to answer the specific questions.)

### Top Leadership

1. Philosophical questions (for example, why have a groups ministry, how small groups fit into the church's ministry "style," application level, extent of use in the church environment, etc.)
2. Selecting the planning team
3. How much authority to delegate to the planning team; to what degree do they want to supervise the ministry?
4. Approving the planning team's plan (goals, structure, and leadership) and budget
5. Evaluating the group ministry's effectiveness based on the church's overall goals

### Planning Team (and Later, the Groups-Ministry Team)

1. How to structure the groups ministry
2. Budget formulation
3. Selecting and training group leaders
4. Further building and promoting the groups ministry
5. Evaluating the overall groups ministry in light of the previously established goals

### Individual Groups

1. Application questions (day, time, place group meets, etc.)
2. Agenda (how the group organizes its time)
3. Procedures (the educational and group methods used)
4. Evaluating their own group's objectives and aims

## CLARIFYING AUTHORITY

Clarifying your authority involves answering three fundamental but vital questions: (1) Who says you can plan a small-groups ministry for your church? (2) What authority (power) do you have, or what decisions can the planning team make and not make as they plan? (3) If necessary, who must approve the team's plan and/or budget prior to implementing the plan?

To find answers for these questions, first ask your pastor, or if appropriate, an associate pastor. In most cases, you may have already discussed this matter with your pastor prior to selecting the planning team (step 1). But if these individuals don't know, ask them whom you should ask. Hopefully the pastor can steer you in the right direction. If not, try asking the chairman (president, etc.) of your governing board. If all else fails, as a last option, just assume you have whatever authority is needed. Believe me, if you overstep your bounds someone will tell you and you can adjust as necessary.

### Question One: Who Says You Can Plan a Small-Groups Ministry for Your Church?

This "permission" should come from the highest authority in your church. Whether it's the pastor, a certain board, or whoever, be sure to identify and follow whatever process is necessary to secure their approval. In doing so, you'll avoid a lot of objections later. It's important from the very beginning to make certain everyone who needs to know does in fact know and approves the idea that you are planning a groups ministry.

### Question Two: What Authority (Power) Do You Have, or What Decisions Can the Planning Team Make and Not Make as They Plan?

In asking for authority clarification, be prepared to describe the type or level of authority you think you'll need in planning the groups ministry. The two basic types of decisions the planning team faces, discussed previously, are a good place to start. In addition, you should have a fairly clear picture of what to request after you've reviewed the material in this handbook. Furthermore, the worksheet at the end of this chapter provides some alternatives.

### Question Three: If Necessary, Who Must Approve the Team's Plan and/or Budget Prior to Implemention?

Question three really fits in question two, but it's so vital I've separated it out for special consideration. In most cases, the pastor or board who approves planning a groups ministry will also want to approve any final plan and budget prior to beginning. Talking about and planning for small groups is okay in many people's minds. But before actually implementing your plan, you're smart to have the key church leaders approve it.

### AUTHORITY CONTACT

One final question related to authority needs asking: Who is your contact? That is, as you exercise whatever authority you are granted, by whomever grants it, you'll need to have a liaison to whom you go to coordinate decisions. Experience has proven that your contact must have direct access—if you don't personally—to the decisionmakers in your church. This is your spokesperson and key to unlocking the "system" in your church.

A member of the board or pastoral team that granted the "permission" makes the best contact person. Ideally this individual also serves on the planning team—it's much easier that way. If not, you'll need to set up some type of regular contact to keep the person informed. Regular, clear communication is vital.

Does all this sound like "politics" to you? It should, because it is. One dictionary defines "politics" as "the acts or practices of those who seek any position of power, authority, or advantage." This describes exactly what you're doing, but on behalf of all those who would profit from the groups ministry. Politics aren't negative in this case, just a reality.

# STEP TWO WORKSHEET: CLARIFYING AUTHORITY

Church Name: MAIN STREET CHURCH    Date: JUNE 12

2-1. *The person filling out this worksheet:*

Name: ELAINE SWAN (SCRIBE)

2-2. *Who can you ask about the planning team's level of authority?*

Name (individual or group): PASTOR ODEN

2-3. *Who says you can plan a small-groups ministry for your church?*

Name (individual or group): PASTOR ODEN/ELDERS

2-4. *Level of authority granted (check one):*

☐ Level One (no authority)
☒ Level Two (some authority)
☐ Level Three (all authority)

Who granted this authority? (Identify the source, person, etc.) ELDERS

2-5. *What authority (power) do you have, or what decisions can the planning team make and not make as they plan?* (Write "D" on the line in front of the items that are areas in which the planning team can make the final decision, and "ND" in front of those they cannot.)

NO    Begin planning the groups ministry. WITH ELDERS' APPROVAL
D    Conduct a survey to identify small-groups' needs and goals.
NO    Determine how small groups will fit into the church's ministry and programming.
NO    Select the type of groups needed. WITH ELDERS' APPROVAL
D    Determine small-group organizational and operational specifics.
D    Recruit potential small-group leaders.
D    Train potential small-group leaders.
D    Promote and publicize small groups.
D    Formulate a system to provide ongoing small-groups administrative leadership.
D    Evaluate the planning process and the first six months of offering
D    small groups.
D    Formulate a budget.
D    Spend church money. WITH TREASURER'S APPROVAL
D    Other (specify): ELDERS WANT THE PLANNING TEAM TO KEEP THEM INFORMED

2-6. *What specific decisions are reserved for the following individuals?*

Top Leadership: TYPE OF GROUPS
HOW GROUPS FIT INTO OUR CHURCH
Planning Team: ADMINISTRATIVE DETAILS

Individual Groups: MEETING TIME, LOCATION, AGENDA

How did you arrive at your answer to this question? (Briefly explain.)
TALKED WITH PASTOR ODEN AND THE ELDERS
DISCUSSED THE MATTER AT THEIR LAST MEETING

2-7. *If necessary, who must approve the team's plan and/or budget prior to imple-menting the plan?*

Is it necessary to have the plan approved prior to implementation? (Check one.)

☒ Yes
☐ No
☐ I don't know (How will you find out?)

If yes, who must give the needed approval? (Name individual or group.)
ELDERS

Is it necessary to have the budget approved prior to implementation? (Check one.)

☒ Yes
☐ No
☐ I don't know (How will you find out?)

If yes, who must give the needed approval? (Name individual or group.)
ELDERS

2-8. *If you need a contact person to coordinate decisions with the church leadership, who is it?*

Name: DON SWAN                    Telephone: 555-1002

Is the above-named individual a member on the planning team?

☒ Yes
☐ No

2-9. *What other authority issues, if any, related to your specific situation must you resolve?* (Briefly describe the issues and whom you must deal with.)
—THE CHURCH TREASURER WANTS TO HAVE A SAY IN ALL
FINANCIAL MATTERS . . . BUDGET IS STILL TIGHT
—CHECK WITH MR. TAYLOR—THE ELDER RESPONSIBLE FOR
LEADERSHIP AND PERSONNEL—BEFORE RECRUITING GROUP
LEADERS

# STEP TWO WORKSHEET: CLARIFYING AUTHORITY

Church Name: _____ Date: _____

2-1. *The person filling out this worksheet:*

Name: _____

2-2. *Who can you ask about the planning team's level of authority?*

Name (individual or group): _____

2-3. *Who says you can plan a small-groups ministry for your church?*

Name (individual or group): _____

2-4. *Level of authority granted (check one):*

☐ Level One (no authority)
☐ Level Two (some authority)
☐ Level Three (all authority)

Who granted this authority? (Identify the source, person, etc.)

2-5. *What authority (power) do you have, or what decisions can the planning team make and not make as they plan?* (Write "D" on the line in front of the items that are areas in which the planning team can make the final decision, and "ND" in front of those they cannot.)

_____Begin planning the groups ministry.
_____Conduct a survey to identify small-groups' needs and goals.
_____Determine how small groups will fit into the church's ministry and programming.
_____Select the type of groups needed.
_____Determine small-group organizational and operational specifics.
_____Recruit potential small-group leaders.
_____Train potential small-group leaders.
_____Promote and publicize small groups.
_____Formulate a system to provide ongoing small-groups administrative leadership.
_____Evaluate the planning process and the first six months of offering small groups.
_____Formulate a budget.
_____Spend church money.
_____Other (specify):

2-6. *What specific decisions are reserved for the following individuals?*

Top Leadership:

Planning Team:

Individual Groups:

How did you arrive at your answer to this question? (Briefly explain.)

2-7. *If necessary, who must approve the team's plan and/or budget prior to implementing the plan?*

Is it necessary to have the plan approved prior to implementation? (Check one.)

☐ Yes
☐ No
☐ I don't know (How will you find out?)

If yes, who must give the needed approval? (Name individual or group.)

Is it necessary to have the budget approved prior to implementation? (Check one.)

☐ Yes
☐ No
☐ I don't know (How will you find out?)

If yes, who must give the needed approval? (Name individual or group.)

2-8. *If you need a contact person to coordinate decisions with the church leadership, who is it?*

Name:_____ Telephone:_____

Is the above-named individual a member on the planning team?

☐ Yes
☐ No

2-9. *What other authority issues, if any, related to your specific situation must you resolve?* (Briefly describe the issues and whom you must deal with.)

STEP THREE

# UNDERSTANDING YOUR CHURCH

*The mind of man plans his way,*
*But the LORD directs his steps.*
PROVERBS 16:9

**OVERVIEW**—This step is designed to assist you in:

1. Knowing why a context audit is important.

2. Planning and conducting a context audit.

3. Identifying your church's key characteristic that potentially impacts your proposed small-groups ministry.

In steps 1 and 2 you planned to plan. Part of your preplanning was to identify several factors that affect the planning process. Now it's time to turn your attention to various aspects or dynamics within your church that directly or indirectly affect your decisions about the small-groups ministry itself.

Step 3 is an information-gathering step. It provides you with and, hopefully, clarifies vital information relevant to your groups ministry; it helps you understand your church's unique "personality." Just like people, churches are distinct entities. Each has its own identity, history, background, etc. It's important to understand your church's personality. Doing so provides you a background on which to base the many decisions the planning team must make. Consequently, the systematic process to identify your church's personality is called a *context audit*.

## CONTEXT AUDIT

A context audit is the systematic process of identifying and understanding the various interpersonal, organizational, social, historical, and spiritual dimensions that characterize a church. It's a formal procedure aimed at securing information that describes the church's unique characteristics. In short, the goal is to figure out what makes a church—your church—tick. A context audit may focus on one specific program, age group, etc., or on the whole church in general. This handbook assumes you and the planning team are focusing on the whole church.

### WHY IS A CONTEXT AUDIT IMPORTANT?

At some point along the way you may have to defend one or more decisions made by you and/or the planning team. Consequently, the clear rationale provided by a context audit usually proves quite useful. So, a thorough and complete context audit is important for at least four reasons:

1. To identify specific characteristics that, when taken as a whole, constitute your church's distinct personality.
2. To provide a basis for making informed decisions about the group ministry's organization and administration, resulting in a groups ministry tailored to your church's specific needs.
3. To furnish a rationale for explaining to the church leadership and potential participants why certain decisions were made.
4. To serve as a partial basis for evaluating the group ministry's effectiveness.

But is a context audit *really necessary*? No, not really. You can plan a small-groups ministry without doing an audit and no one may even know the difference. Yet the chances of developing a successful small-groups ministry increase in proportion to the amount of time and effort you spend on this critical activity. An audit provides the specific information you need to tailor a small-groups ministry to the unique needs represented in your church. Lastly, a context audit is *highly* recommended if for no other reason than to affirm your planning process and undergird the need for small groups.

## HOW TO CONDUCT A CONTEXT AUDIT

Conducting a context audit can range from a simple procedure to a very complex process. Most churches opt for something in between. Nevertheless, all context audits must deal with four issues: what to ask, how to ask, who to ask, and when to ask.

### What Should Be Asked?

How would you describe your church? What information do you need to plan a realistic, effective small-groups ministry? What questions do you need to ask in order to answer these questions? If you're like me, it's fairly easy to generate a long list of potential questions you'd like to ask. Therefore, whatever other questions you may deem necessary, be sure to include questions that help you to explore the following issues:

CHURCH DEMOGRAPHICS—Knowing the church's age, affiliation, size, location, membership characteristics, etc., is very important, especially when determining what type of groups are best utilized in your context.

YOUR CHURCH'S PREVIOUS HISTORY AND BACKGROUND WITH SMALL GROUPS—Knowing where the church has been helps in knowing where it needs to go. Specifically, it's very useful to find out about any small-groups ministry successes or failures the church has experienced in the past. This information can help you capitalize on previous achievements or avoid repeating past mistakes. Furthermore, information in this area is useful in understanding the "mind-set" or attitude toward small groups—pro or con—you'll encounter among the church members and leaders.

THE AMOUNT OF SUPPORT YOUR PASTOR AND CHURCH LEADERS HAVE FOR A SMALL-GROUPS MINISTRY—Do your pastor and other church leaders favor starting a small-groups ministry? Are they convinced small groups are vital, necessary for your church? You need to know the answer to these questions because if you're a layperson who is highly interested in small groups, but your pastor and church leaders are uninterested or indifferent, you have a difficult "sales job" ahead of you.

THE LEADERSHIP CONTEXT IN WHICH THE GROUPS MINISTRY MUST EXIST AND OPERATE—Every church has a ministry or leadership context that affects how church programs are planned and how they operate. In some churches lay leaders have complete freedom to do as they see fit. In other churches lay leaders must merely do as they are told. Authority and control are central concepts in both extremes. The amount of control the pastor or church board exercises must be identified.

THE NEEDS EXISTING WITHIN THE CHURCH THAT ARE APPROACHABLE THROUGH A SMALL-GROUPS MINISTRY—While step 5 deals with this issue in detail, at this point it's important to note that most context audits routinely uncover needs, in all shapes and sizes, existing within the church. Sorting through them and determining which can be addressed in or by small groups is the goal. You'll discover all needs cannot be met by small groups.

## How Do You Ask?

You have several vehicles through which to conduct a useful context audit in and for your church (adult class, choir, organizations, etc.). From one-person audits to large-scale audits, three basic methods are possible:

INDIVIDUAL AUDIT—The quickest but least accurate method is to have one person conduct the audit (a pastor, elder, planning team member, etc.). Relying on personal experience, this individual answers the audit questions and secures the necessary information without involving anyone else. This method works in limited situations. A do-it-yourself audit is especially useful when time is limited and you must make decisions in short order. However, you may be surprised at how limited one person's knowledge is or how he or she doesn't know where to find needed information.

COLLABORATIVE AUDIT—Teamwork is best. The planning team, working together, can conduct the audit as one of their first tasks. To start, have the team determine what information or questions are needed. Then divide them up into subteams to seek out and obtain the necessary information. Later have the team meet to share their findings and complete the audit questionnaire that appears later in this section.

SURVEY AUDIT—A third option is to conduct a survey among the adult members/regular attenders in your church. However, rarely can a survey provide you with all the audit information you need. Therefore, when used, a survey is usually just one part in a context audit. Surveys are especially useful in determining church leaders' and adult participants' attitudes toward small groups and identifying the existing needs small groups can seek to meet (see step 4).

## Who Do You Ask?

The question you want answered makes a big difference in who you ask. Rarely can any one individual answer every question in a context audit. In fact, in some cases you don't have to ask anyone at all. Church records can provide lots of useful information.

A good strategy is to ask the church clerk (or whatever your church calls the individual who maintains the church records) for any factual, historical information. Ask older members serving on your governing board for information on the history of small groups in the church. Ask your pastor how he or she feels about a small-groups ministry. In short, most information you need is readily available; you just have to find the right person to ask. In some cases it may mean asking more than one person or group, so be sure to budget enough time to contact all the people from whom you need to secure information.

## When Do You Ask?

Someone said that timing is everything. I agree. Avoid waiting until the last minute—the night before the day it's needed—to ask for opinions or information. It's a good idea to make up a schedule to guide the information-gathering process. Once the team has determined what information it needs, a schedule can prove very useful in collecting the information in a timely manner.

A context-audit schedule should include: (1) what information is needed, (2) who is responsible to secure it, (3) the intended source, and (4) the deadline date for acquiring the information. But remember, the schedule is only a guide, not a rigid requirement.

## A CONTEXT-AUDIT TOOL

A context-audit instrument is provided below. It's a generic tool suitable for most churches. However, as with everything in this handbook, please add or subtract anything that makes it more useful in your context and situation.

The audit tool is intended for use by the planning team. It provides a series of questions designed to solicit answers that, in turn, provide information that will be useful during later steps in the planning process. No direct link between certain questions and specific planning steps is intended. The resulting information, however, provides insightful background that is useful in making numerous decisions.

Below is one strategy for utilizing the tool. You're free, of course, to make any adjustments you deem necessary to tailor it to your specific situation and needs:

1. Review the questions to determine what additional questions, if any, are needed and what information you need to answer the selected questions.
2. Determine which questions team members can answer themselves and which require answers from outside sources.
3. Divide the planning team into subteams and distribute the questions needing additional information among the subteams. Decide where to obtain the needed information.
4. Set a schedule and deadlines for the subteams to follow in acquiring the information.
5. Schedule a meeting where the team pools the information and summarizes the overall audit results.
6. In light of the collected information, discuss any significant findings and how the data impacts your future small-groups ministry.

In some cases the context audit may be combined with the needs assessment described in step 5. Whether you do this will depend on available resources—time, money, and people. However, in most situations the context audit and the needs assessment are two distinct activities associated with building a small-groups ministry.

## SMALL-GROUPS CHURCH CONTEXT AUDIT

Completing this checklist gives you a good picture of certain characteristics and dynamics in your church that influence your present and/or future groups ministry.

This isn't a test, but accuracy is important. Make sure to budget enough time—about thirty minutes—to complete the entire checklist.

Note: The checklist is worded in a manner appropriate for conducting an audit for your whole church. However, if you're only dealing with one adult class, organization, etc., just read in the appropriate term every time you read "church."

*Instructions:* Check the most appropriate answer or provide a written response for each item.

### CHURCH DEMOGRAPHICS

1. How old is your church/parish?  _____Years old

2. Which of the following categories best describes your church/parish identity? (check one)

☐ Independent
☐ Protestant denomination or association
☐ Roman Catholic
☐ Other (please specify):

3. How large is your church (adult or family members/regular attenders; circle the category used)?

_____Adults or families

4. On average, how many adults attend your Sunday (or whatever day) morning worship service(s)?

_____ Adults

5. Where is your church/parish located?

☐ In a city/urban setting with a population of
☐ In the suburbs with a population of
☐ In a rural town with a population of
☐ In a rural/country setting
☐ Other (please specify):

6. Which of the following best describes your church/parish's governing system (polity)?

☐ "Congregational" (Baptist, Brethren, Evangelical Free, Mennonite, Independent, etc.)
☐ "Episcopal" (Methodist, Episcopalian, Orthodox, Roman Catholic, etc.)
☐ "Presbyterian" (Presbyterian, Reformed, etc.)
☐ Other (please specify):
☐ I don't know

7. Generally speaking, estimate the percentage of adults in your church who fit into each of the following age categories (should add up to 100 percent):

_____ 18-39 years old
_____ 40-59 years old
_____ 60-79 years old
_____ 80 or older

8. Generally speaking, which of the following economic categories best describes the majority of adults who regularly attend your church?

☐ Upper class, affluent
☐ Upper middle class, successful
☐ Middle class, comfortable
☐ Lower middle class, modest
☐ Lower class, limited financial resources
☐ A mix of the above
☐ Other (please specify):

9. What percentage of adults active in your church fit into each of the following educational categories (should add up to 100 percent)?

_____ Completed less than high school
_____ Completed high school
_____ Completed trade school or some college
_____ Completed an associate's or bachelor's degree
_____ Completed graduate or professional education

10. What is the size of your pastoral staff (all categories; write the numbers)?

_____ Ordained
_____ Nonordained

11. How many support staff (secretarial, custodial, etc.) does your church employ?

_____ Full-time people
_____ Part-time people

12. If asked, how would you describe your church and its members/attenders to a friend who doesn't attend the church? (Write your description.)

## CHURCH'S SMALL-GROUPS HISTORY

13. During the past ten years has your church offered any kind of small-groups ministry?

☐ Yes
☐ No (Skip questions 14 through 16)
☐ I don't know (Find out, but skip questions 14 through 16)

14. Does your church currently offer any type of small-groups ministry?
☐ Yes
☐ No
☐ I don't know

15. Which of the following phrases best describes the kinds of small groups included in your church's present small-groups ministry?
☐ One kind (type or format) of small groups
☐ Several kinds (types or formats) of small groups
☐ I don't know

16. Which of the following statements best describes how small groups fit into your church?
☐ They're considered a vital part of our church.
☐ They're considered important, but not vital.
☐ They're just another program among many.
☐ They're tolerated, but not encouraged.

17. Which of the following phrases, in your opinion, best describes the success (given how *you* define "success") of your church's present small-groups ministry?
☐ Great success
☐ Moderate success
☐ Less than desired success

### Attitudes Toward Small Groups

Read each statement in this section, and then circle the number on the continuum that best represents your level of agreement.

18. I think small groups are a necessary ministry in my church.

| Strongly Agree | | | | | Strongly Disagree | Undecided | I Don't Know |
|---|---|---|---|---|---|---|---|
| 1 | 2 | 3 | 4 | 5 | 6 | 7 | 8 |

19. The "formal church leadership" (pastors, elders, deacons, etc.) for the most part think small groups are a necessary ministry in our church.

| Strongly Agree | | | | | Strongly Disagree | Undecided | I Don't Know |
|---|---|---|---|---|---|---|---|
| 1 | 2 | 3 | 4 | 5 | 6 | 7 | 8 |

20. My senior pastor (if not myself) thinks small groups are a necessary ministry in our church.

| Strongly Agree | | | | | Strongly Disagree | Undecided | I Don't Know |
|---|---|---|---|---|---|---|---|
| 1 | 2 | 3 | 4 | 5 | 6 | 7 | 8 |

21. My church's adult members/attenders, in general, think small groups are a necessary ministry in our church.

| Strongly Agree | | | | | Strongly Disagree | Undecided | I Don't Know |
|---|---|---|---|---|---|---|---|

| 1 | 2 | 3 | 4 | 5 | 6 | 7 | 8 |
|---|---|---|---|---|---|---|---|

22. What objections—if any—do you think you'll encounter among church members if a small-groups ministry is offered? (Use back if more space is needed.)

### LEADERSHIP CONTEXT

23. Thinking about the amount of "authority" the pastor (or pastoral staff) exercises over your church's ministries in general, which statement is most accurate?

☐ Complete authority (all or nearly all decisions affecting our various church ministries are made by the pastor).
☐ Moderate authority (many, but not all, decisions are made by the pastor; specific ministry leaders have some power to make certain, limited decisions).
☐ Little authority (only limited decisions are made by the pastor; specific ministry leaders make most decisions affecting their ministries).
☐ No authority (specific ministry leaders are free to make all the decisions affecting their ministries without consulting the pastor).

24. What groups or individuals, other than the pastor or pastoral staff, are the decisionmakers when it comes to establishing or continuing small groups in your church? Rank your answers in terms of their importance (list the most important first, the second most important, etc.).

25. Who is (or would be) accountable for providing the vision and leadership needed to establish a small-groups ministry in your church?

☐ The church board, council, presbytery, etc.
☐ The senior pastor
☐ An associate/assistant pastor
☐ A layperson
☐ A group of laypersons
☐ A group of laypersons and pastor(s)
☐ Other (please specify):

26. Who is (or would be) responsible for overseeing the day-to-day administration of your church's small groups?

☐ The senior pastor
☐ An associate/assistant pastor
☐ A layperson
☐ A group of laypersons
☐ A group of laypersons and pastor(s)
☐ Other (please specify):

27. Complete the following sentence in your own words: "My (or the planning team's) role in planning and establishing a small groups ministry is to . . ."

28. A final catchall question: In general, what other things, people, conditions, etc., within your church—but not yet mentioned—do you think affect planning, introducing, and implementing a small-groups ministry?

# STEP THREE WORKSHEET: UNDERSTANDING YOUR CHURCH

Church Name: _MAIN STREET CHURCH_      Date: _____

3-1. *The person filling out this worksheet:*

     Name: _ELAINE SWAN (SCRIBE)_____

3-2. *Is the small-groups ministry team (or equivalent) responsible for conducting the context audit?*

     ☒ Yes    _PLANNING TEAM WILL DIVIDE UP THE TASK_
     ☐ No; then please specify who is responsible and describe how the various responsibilities are divided up:

3-3. *What method is used to conduct the context audit?* (Check the appropriate option.)

     ☐ Individual audit; please specify the person:

     ☒ A collaborative audit; please describe: _DIVIDE INTO THREE TASKS:_
_D.SWAN, ADAMS—PASTOR AND LEADERSHIP SUPPORT_
_E. SWAN, HOWE—CHURCH'S EXISTING NEEDS*_
_EDGAR—CHURCH DEMOGRAPHICS AND BACKGROUND_
_WITH SMALL GROUP_

                               _*SWAN AND HOWE WILL DEVELOP_
                               _A SHORT "NEEDS_
     ☐ Survey audit; please describe:    _SURVEY"_

     ☐ Other; please explain:

3-4 *Is the "Small-Groups Church Context Audit" provided in this handbook adequate for your needs?*

☐ Yes, it's adequate the way it is.
☒ Yes, but with the following changes: THE AUDIT TOOL WILL BE USED BY THE PLANNING TEAM . . . A SECOND SURVEY TOOL IS BEING DEVELOPED TO USE WITH THE ADULT MEMBERS

☐ No, we plan to develop a new one (please describe):

3-5. *Who do you ask?* (Identify the person or persons who will supply the needed information.)
—PASTOR AND ELDERS (OPINIONS, EXPECTATIONS)
—CHURCH CLERK (RECORDS, ETC.)
—ADULT MEMBERS (OPINIONS)

3-6. *When do you ask—what is the context-audit schedule?* (Please specify.)
X SCHEDULE TIME AT AN ELDERS' MEETING (MAY 18)
X SCHEDULE A MEETING WITH PASTOR ODEN (LUNCH, MAY 16)
X SURVEY IN ADULT EDUCATION CLASSES (JUNE 5, 12)
    AND MORNING SERVICE (JUNE 12)

# STEP THREE WORKSHEET: UNDERSTANDING YOUR CHURCH

Church Name: _____ Date: _____

3-1. *The person filling out this worksheet:*

Name: _____

3-2. *Is the small-groups ministry team (or equivalent) responsible for conducting the context audit?*

☐ Yes
☐ No; then please specify who is responsible and describe how the various responsibilities are divided up:

3-3. *What method is used to conduct the context audit?* (Check the appropriate option.)

☐ Individual audit; please specify the person:

☐ A collaborative audit; please describe:

☐ Survey audit; please describe:

☐ Other; please explain:

3-4 *Is the "Small-Groups Church Context Audit" provided in this handbook adequate for your needs?*

☐ Yes, it's adequate the way it is.
☐ Yes, but with the following changes:

☐ No, we plan to develop a new one (please describe):

3-5. *Who do you ask?* (Identify the person or persons who will supply the needed information.)

3-6. *When do you ask—what is the context-audit schedule?* (Please specify.)

# STEP FOUR
# DETERMINING MINISTRY "FIT"

*A plan in the heart of man is like deep water,*
*But a man of understanding draws it out.*
PROVERBS 20:5

**OVERVIEW**—This step is designed to assist you in:

1. Determining which church classification best describes your church.

2. Sorting through competitive or cooperative, supervised or nonsupervised, structured or nonstructured options for your groups ministry.

3. Defining decisionmaking responsibilities.

4. Clarifying your church's "style" and the "application level" suitable for your groups ministry.

5. Deciding which small-groups-ministry "path" best fits your situation.

**H**ow do small groups fit into your church's philosophy of adult ministries, or its philosophy of ministry in general? Are groups an integral part, a vital element, a necessary component in discipling your adult members, or just one alternative among many good programs adults can choose to participate in?

This step is intended to help you identify how small groups "fit" into your church's adult ministries. Small-groups ministries don't enjoy the same status or significance within all churches. Some churches view groups as inherent to how they define the church, while others relegate groups to merely one programming option among many. Most churches probably fit somewhere in between these two extremes. However, my experience has taught me that the majority of churches that offer small-groups ministries fit on one of three planes. The chart on the next page depicts what I'm talking about.

The names "Traditional Church," "Transitional Church," and "Transformational Church" aren't inspired. Use whatever names make sense to you. Nonetheless, the three planes or categories are different ways of looking at and describing small-groups ministries existing in today's churches.

The traditional church possesses a conventional outlook in most areas, including small groups. These are "typical" churches familiar to most people. Usually older, well-established congregations, they maintain a programmatic "canon" just as fixed and unchanging as the biblical canon. If small groups are included in the programmatic mix, they aren't central to the church's identity or function. At best, the groups include only 10 to 15 percent of the adult members. There is no expectation placed on adult members to participate. No effort is made to integrate groups into the church's essential identity; groups are merely one programmatic option. Furthermore, pastoral support and leadership, if any, are very passive.

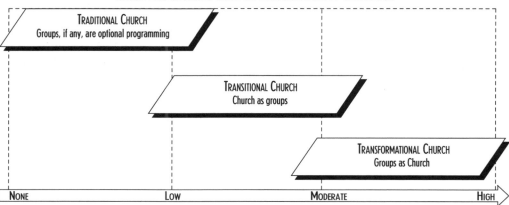

CLASSIFYING CHURCHES BASED ON THEIR SMALL-GROUP ORIENTATION

Freedom and/or likelihood of experimenting with programs and methods

TRADITIONAL CHURCH—
Groups are one programmatic option; groups must compete for resources and participants; groups are not viewed as essential to the nature or functioning of a local church; group membership is purely optional; none to moderate pastoral support for groups.

TRANSITIONAL CHURCH—
Groups are an integral part of the church; group membership is highly encouraged, if not expected; groups are viewed as being essential to the nature and functioning of the church; strong pastoral support for groups.

TRANSFORMATIONAL CHURCH—
Church identity is focused in groups or house churches; group membership is equated with church membership; groups are the nature of and how the church functions; pastoral leadership focused on group facilitation.

---

Transitional churches possess many traditional church characteristics and programming elements, but they aren't locked into a traditional mind-set. The biggest difference is in how they view small groups. Churches in this category embrace groups as a vital, integral part of how they view and operate their church. Adult members aren't necessarily required to participate, but everyone is strongly encouraged to join a group. Strong pastoral support is a key. The pastor and/or pastoral team enthusiastically promote and participate in the groups ministry.

Transformational churches are radical by today's church standards, but not so by biblical standards. They see "church" from a totally different perspective. Small groups aren't just part of the church, they *are* the church! In fact, group membership equates to church membership, not the other way around. *Everyone* is in a group. Groups are how the church functions. The contemporary house-church movement is a good example of the transformational church strategy. Pastors are, first of all, small-groups facilitators and leaders, and secondly, large-group leaders—when more than one small group meets together for worship, education, etc.

Even though these categories are generalizations, *which category best describes your church?* Most likely it's a traditional church or a church wanting to become a transitional church. I doubt you'd be reading this handbook if you were in a transformational church. Churches in this category aren't interested in building a groups ministry because they already exist as small groups. *Consequently, from this point on this handbook focuses on building small-group ministries in and for traditional churches and churches wanting to adopt a transformational identity.*

But first, let me share with you some additional observations based on my experience. In the next section you'll discover four stages many churches go through in developing effective group ministries. Once again, they're useful generalizations designed to help you think through your own situation.

## ORGANIZATIONAL DEVELOPMENT STAGES IN SMALL-GROUPS MINISTRIES

While associated with Serendipity (a national small-groups ministry), I developed a classification system that describes the fairly predictable life cycle traditional or transitional churches often go through in their attempts to formulate and offer a small-groups ministry. Four distinct but interrelated stages are customary. But a cautionary word is needed at this point. The suggested stages are only generalizations. Not every groups ministry goes through all four stages, nor do the stages accurately describe all situations. It's quite possible for a groups ministry to exist somewhere in between two or more stages or to fit none of the stages at all. Furthermore, knowing that the different stages commonly exist, a church can elect to skip one or more stages. Enough said. Here are the stages:

STAGE ONE: DEBUT ("DO YOUR OWN THING")—Stage one often occurs in one of two situations: (1) Small-groups ministry is not a formal church program; groups meet on their own initiative and determine their own agenda; often a "grass-roots" program without pastoral leadership; decisions based on the Judges Principle: *"Everyone did what was right in his own eyes"* (Judges 21:25); or (2) small groups are recognized by the church and pastor, but not a formal program; minimal organizational assistance; groups determine their own agenda.

STAGE TWO: DEFINITION ("THE PROGRAM")—Well-organized, highly prescriptive small-groups ministry sponsored by the church; "the" program offered for all adults in the church; strong, centralized decisionmaking; a definite desire to integrate groups into vision and ministry.

STAGE THREE: DIVERSITY ("SMORGASBORD")—Well-organized, flexible small-groups ministry; multiple small-group formats based on various needs; shared, decentralized decisionmaking; small groups integral to ministry philosophy.

STAGE FOUR: DECLINE ("A PROGRAM")—Well-organized but deteriorating small-groups ministry; operating at any stage; loss of vision, becoming just another program; lack of constructive evaluation; often caused by a change in pastoral leadership.

A healthy stage three, in most cases, represents the ideal small-groups ministry suitable for most churches, especially large churches. This doesn't mean the other stages should be avoided. On the contrary, all but the last stage—stage four—are real options.

GENERALIZATIONS ABOUT ORGANIZATIONAL DEVELOPMENT STAGES IN A GROUPS-MINISTRY LIFE CYCLE

| CHARACTERISTICS | STAGE ONE: DEBUT | STAGE TWO: DEFINITION | STAGE THREE: DIVERSITY | STAGE FOUR: DECLINE |
|---|---|---|---|---|
| Level of organizational structure | No formal structure or program | Well-defined and centralized | Defined, flexible, and decentralized | Complex, loss of definition |
| "Ownership" of groups by church | Not recognized or minimal recognition | High recognition, "the" small-groups program | High recognition, "our" small-group opportunities | Recognized, but a secondary emphasis/ program |
| Control and decision-making | Internal, each group decides for itself | External, church groups-ministry leaders and/or pastoral leadership | Internal and external, shared; strong pastoral leadership | Internal and external, indifferent; change in pastoral leadership |
| Group leader's accountability | Within the individual group, little or no assistance from the church | To the groups-ministry leadership, precise directions from the church | To the groups-ministry leadership, focus on leadership training | To the groups-ministry leadership, but increasing independence |
| Communication process and planning | Informal, little or no formal planning | Formal, centralized planning | Moderately formal, shared planning based on needs | Extremes, formal to highly informal; lack of evaluation |
| Perceived contribution to church "success" | Little or no contribution, not part of ministry philosophy | Important contribution, emerging in ministry philosophy | Vital contribution, integral to ministry philosophy | Taken for granted, one of many important programs |
| Church/groups growth rate | Inconsistent but improving | Positive growth, very rapid growth in some cases | Growth stable or beginning to plateau | Plateaued or beginning to decline |
| Church/groups age and size | Young and small and/or new to groups | Larger and established or new to groups | Largest or once large and well established | Larger and well established |

## COMPETITION OR COOPERATION

There is an important question dealing with programmatic philosophy that needs your attention early in the planning process. Namely, where does your potential groups ministry fit on the competition/cooperation continuum?

As you plan, it's vital for you to understand how the groups ministry fits into what the church is already doing, how it blends with or stands apart from other adult-ministry programming elements. Two extremes are possible: competition or cooperation. These two contrary positions exist at opposite ends of a continuum. To one far side is *total competition*. This extreme represents a situation where all the adult programs in a church are separate, unrelated structures or organizations. Each operates totally independently and "competes" with each other for recognition, financial resources, and participants from among the adult members. No effort is made to coordinate the various activities—or even the number of activities—sponsored by the separate organizations, especially in larger churches. A coherent ministry philosophy is absent. Consequently, the programs end up—unintentionally—competing with one other. People are forced to view the situation as a programmatic smorgasbord from which they choose a little of this program, a little of that program, and none of some programs.

COMPETITION            COOPERATION

Total Competition    Competitive    Cooperative    Total Cooperation

At the continuum's opposite side is *total cooperation*. This is usually thought of as a desirable condition; however, here I'm referring to extreme efforts focused on absolute cooperation in everything. Wanting to avoid the competitive dilemma, every program is rigidly structured and monitored. Church leaders restrict the number of programs offered and stress total participation by all adult members in those that are offered. Organizations are highly controlled by the pastor or governing board in order to ensure against competitive ministry philosophies and activities. Financial resources are equally divided among the organizational elements. A major goal is to coordinate and cooperate in everything done in the church, from children's ministries on up through the senior-citizen activities.

Neither extreme is desirable in most cases. However, finding the right balance between the two extremes is tricky. We humans, even as Christians, tend to drift toward extreme positions; it's easier, more clear-cut. Finding the right programmatic balance in our churches takes work. Yet, it's this elusive equilibrium that provides the best context for small-group ministries.

I prefer a "cooperative" church context: a moderated position that encourages cooperation but recognizes that total cooperation is both unnecessary and unrealistic. Likewise, total competition is considered unhealthy for and in the Body of Christ. Only in limited circumstances are competitive programs deemed acceptable (for personal achievement, athletic events, youth outings, etc.), but never as a ministry or programmatic characteristic.

## SUPERVISION AND STRUCTURE

Two additional considerations—*supervision* and *structure*—demand your attention as you think about how your groups ministry fits into your church's style and operation.

### Supervision

Related to authority, which we discussed back in step 1 with reference to the planning team, "supervision" refers to how much your pastor, pastoral staff, or governing board want to oversee the direction of and leadership in the groups ministry. It's a control issue. How much control do they want to assert? The possibilities range on a continuum from complete supervision to no supervision.

SUPERVISION            NON-SUPERVISION

Complete Supervision    Some Supervision    Minimal Supervision    No Supervision

COMPLETE SUPERVISION—The pastors (or board members) view themselves as running the groups ministry (and everything else); all decisions are centralized and affect all groups; some, but very few, routine decisions are made by groups-ministry leaders and individual groups.

*SOME SUPERVISION*—Supervision boundaries are spelled out; most substantive decisions are centralized; groups-ministry leaders and individual groups make only limited routine decisions.

*MINIMAL SUPERVISION*—Limited informal supervision is provided on an informal basis; very few decisions are centralized; groups-ministry leaders make most substantive and routine decisions.

*NO SUPERVISION*—The pastors or board provides no supervision; oversight isn't wanted or required; groups-ministry leaders operate on their own in making substantive and routine decisions; individual groups make many routine decisions.

Your context audit (see step 3, question 23, page 38, on the "Small-Groups Church Context Audit") should give you a pretty good feel for how much or how little supervision is relevant in your context. For example, if your pastor is ranked as being in "complete authority," it's almost certain "complete supervision" is likely. This means your groups ministry must be designed to fit into a context and operation where the pastor is certain to take a very directive hand in determining what type of groups are needed, who leads them, and what the groups do. If on the other hand your pastor is rated "no authority," it follows that you are working in a "no supervision" context.

## Structure

Every groups ministry has a structure: the organizational systems and methods that define how the ministry is built. Structure provides organization. Some churches prefer highly structured, well-organized group ministries; others prefer as little structure as possible, or none at all. Once again, a continuum is useful in depicting how groups ministries can vary from totally structured to completely nonstructured.

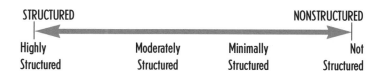

STRUCTURED                                          NONSTRUCTURED

Highly                    Moderately        Minimally           Not
Structured                Structured        Structured          Structured

*HIGHLY STRUCTURED*—Highly organized groups ministry; little or no flexibility, all groups fit into a defined system and operate in a similar manner.

*MODERATELY STRUCTURED*—Most structural decisions are predetermined by the groups-ministry team; limited organizational options are available for individual groups to make.

*MINIMALLY STRUCTURED*—Minimal organizational structures are required by the groups-ministry team; individual groups have some freedom to organize themselves.

*NOT STRUCTURED*—No formal organizational structure is required; individual groups are totally free to organize themselves as they please.

*How much structure do you want to impose on your groups ministry?* An answer to this question usually requires determining how much authority your church leadership, and secondly, the groups-ministry leadership, wants to have over the ministry's philosophical issues and functional operations—in short, the amount of authority they wish to exercise. Churches with high-authority leadership tend toward highly structured groups ministries. But a church has the choice to formulate a groups ministry anywhere along the structure continuum. This choice, however, usually is made by "top" leadership (pastors and governing boards), not those charged with planning and running the groups ministry. Yet, this latter group carries the day-to-day responsibility to devise and implement the groups ministry based on however much authority they are granted. Consequently, it's time to specifically address who makes what decisions in a groups ministry.

## CHURCH STYLE

Your church, and every church, has a distinct personality. Understanding its general personality was your goal back in step 3. One additional, specific personality dimension now comes into focus: your church's "style." Your church has a ministry style—the type of ministry it's best known for, its dominant ministry form and reputation. Some churches are evangelistic, some are known for their teaching ministries, others have developed a reputation for social peace and justice, and still others are known for helping those who are down and out. Can you think of other styles for which churches are known?

To succeed, a groups ministry must be compatible, fitting into the church's style. In fact, the correctly applied groups ministries not only reflect the church's style, but in most cases they help to establish and make it well known. For example, one church I'm familiar with in Oregon is known as a "helping" church. Their "main-path" (a topic coming up shortly) small-groups ministry concentrates on assisting group members to deal with spiritual and personal struggles. As a result, besides serving church members, many nonChristians are attracted to the church through their groups ministry.

How do you determine your church's style? In many cases, it's straightforward—everyone already knows. In other situations you'll need to ask your pastor, individuals on the church governing board, or longstanding church members. Don't be surprised if you get a blank stare. You may have to explain what you're asking. If you have no luck, ask one or two individuals who pastor other churches in your community—they'll surely know.

Applying what you know about your church's style to making decisions required in designing a groups ministry isn't a simple one-two-three process. The procedure entails utilizing your understanding as a background or information base for sorting through and selecting between programmatic structures and options. It's a "fuzzy" process involving a whole lot of "art" and not very much "science" (this art and science analogy appears again in step 5). Nevertheless, maybe the following three statements/guidelines can help:

1. What are your church's key ministry characteristics, its style?
2. What type or types of groups best fit into this style (step 6 deals with types of groups)?
3. Is the groups ministry designed to complement, contrast, or establish an entirely new style for your church?

## APPLICATION LEVELS

Small groups are a useful ministry tool applicable at many different levels. Not every church, consequently, offers a churchwide groups ministry from the very beginning. Some elect to start their group ministries within a specific, smaller segment of their congregation or community. Frequently the segment or suborganization focused on is adult education—all the adult-education (Sunday school) classes, or even one specific class.

Furthermore, it's realistic to focus only on women, men, or one particular age group (young marrieds, senior adults, etc.). One church even started with their elder board (a good "modeling" option).

There are advantages to starting small and focused. Investing a year or two in "pilot testing" various group strategies and options in one adult class, age group, etc., gives you the chance to find out what works best in your context. In addition, doing so can provide an opportunity to enlist and train leaders to later help you expand the program. But perhaps the best reason, especially if your church has a negative history with small groups, is to build a committed corps of "groupies." These folks become your best salespeople when it comes to proclaiming the need for and benefits of small groups.

What application level fits your situation? Is it better to start small and expand, or just launch into a groups ministry that attempts to include all the adult members/attenders in your church? Answers to these questions must come from deliberations with the top leaders in your church.

The application question surfaces again in step 5 when you do a needs assessment and write the goals for your groups ministry. But for now, I need to introduce a new topic related to application levels—groups-ministry "paths."

## GROUPS MINISTRY "PATHS"

We are now ready to talk about "paths" within group ministries. I didn't use the term earlier in the chapter, but you already read something about group-ministry paths. The first two stages—definition and diversity—under "Organizational Development Stages in Small-Groups Ministries" (page 47) partly mirror two different paths or options commonly found in small-group ministries (refer to the following chart). The first option is what I call "the main path." In this case the groups ministry is a well-defined structured or nonstructured program aimed at including all the adult members in the church or in a church segment. It's the program most people are referring to when they tell a friend about the groups ministry in their church. A main-path groups ministry is based on common goals shared by all the groups. The individual groups may vary in functional details, but as a whole they are the same "type" of group.

The second option, "specialty paths," utilizes diverse groups that exist to meet similar or completely dissimilar needs. There is a wide range of goals directing the different group options. Consequently, specialty-path groups focus more narrowly on specific needs and interests. Often these groups address serious social and spiritual needs (for example, recovery groups, support groups, etc.). Church members may or may not need or want to participate. While everyone is invited, no effort is made to have everyone attend. Groups on this path meet on both a short-term and a long-term basis. However, frequently long-term groups have a regular, planned turnover in group membership. In some cases specialty groups are low-level group therapy led by a professional. Specialty-path groups are often excellent tools for reaching out and ministering to the church's community.

You should seriously consider both options. Some churches, depending on "fit" decisions, may want to offer only one path type. Others may find it preferable to go down both paths at the same time. One good option is to start with a main-path program and branch out with specialty paths at a later date, or reverse the order and start with specialty groups first.

Large, group-oriented churches normally offer both path options. The diversity among those attending a large church usually makes this necessary.

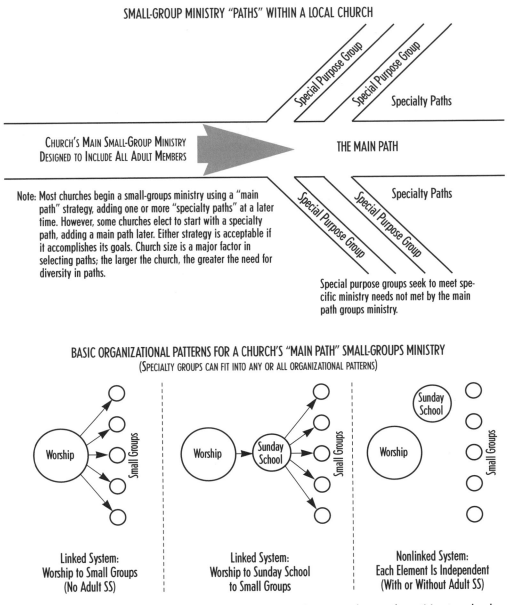

SMALL-GROUP MINISTRY "PATHS" WITHIN A LOCAL CHURCH

Special Purpose Group
Special Purpose Group

Specialty Paths

CHURCH'S MAIN SMALL-GROUP MINISTRY DESIGNED TO INCLUDE ALL ADULT MEMBERS

THE MAIN PATH

Specialty Paths

Special Purpose Group
Special Purpose Group

Note: Most churches begin a small-groups ministry using a "main path" strategy, adding one or more "specialty paths" at a later time. However, some churches elect to start with a specialty path, adding a main path later. Either strategy is acceptable if it accomplishes its goals. Church size is a major factor in selecting paths; the larger the church, the greater the need for diversity in paths.

Special purpose groups seek to meet specific ministry needs not met by the main path groups ministry.

BASIC ORGANIZATIONAL PATTERNS FOR A CHURCH'S "MAIN PATH" SMALL-GROUPS MINISTRY
(SPECIALTY GROUPS CAN FIT INTO ANY OR ALL ORGANIZATIONAL PATTERNS)

Worship — Small Groups

Linked System:
Worship to Small Groups
(No Adult SS)

Worship — Sunday School — Small Groups

Linked System:
Worship to Sunday School
to Small Groups

Sunday School — Worship — Small Groups

Nonlinked System:
Each Element Is Independent
(With or Without Adult SS)

The term linked describes a recognized and promoted connection between the program elements, the participants, and perhaps the content. Linked and nonlinked systems reflect different ministry philosophies.

## To Link or Not to Link

The word *link* is used to describe a deliberate relationship forged between the groups ministry and other significant adult ministries, such as the weekly worship service and adult education (note chart above). Linked systems recognize and promote philosophical and practical connections between the program elements, the participants, and perhaps the content. Conversely, you may opt for a nonlinked groups ministry. In this option the worship services, educational ministries, and group ministries all exist as independent programs. No effort is made to coordinate the ministry elements.

Perhaps an illustration would help. Look at the center section on the chart that appears on the previous page, "Linked System: Worship to Sunday School to Small Groups." This linked option illustrates a cooperative system where adult members are subdivided into adult-education classes, which are further subdivided into small groups. In some instances the same content, but from different perspectives, is used at all three levels: a biblical passage is preached on in the morning service; the same passage is systematically studied in adult-education classes, with a discussion on possible applications; the small groups then focus on applying that same passage to their individual and corporate lives. When successfully implemented, this system boasts the support and promotion of the church's pastoral staff and lay leadership. A more complete explanation appears in the appendixes.

Linked group ministries are more difficult to establish and maintain than nonlinked ministries. Why? It goes back to competition or cooperation. Cooperative linked systems consume more time, demand more planning, and require extensive coordination. Church leadership often doesn't have the time and training (or inclination) to meet these expectations. Thus, nonlinked systems are more common.

## PUTTING IT ALL TOGETHER
The first four steps in this planning process deal with preplanning and necessary background information. Now it's time to put it all together and begin planning the actual small-groups ministry. The remaining steps—5 through 12—will take you through a process designed to apply the first four steps in building a groups ministry tailored to your own context and situation.

# STEP FOUR WORKSHEET: DETERMINING MINISTRY "FIT"

Church Name: __MAIN STREET CHURCH__    Date: _____

4-1. *The person filling out this worksheet:*

   Name: ___ELAINE SWAN___

4-2. *Which classification best describes your church when it comes to its small-groups orientation?* (Check one.)

   ☒ Traditional church    ☐ Transitional church    ☐ Transformational church

   Briefly explain your reasons for checking this category:
   X 30 YEARS OLD
   X "TRADITIONAL" PROGRAMMING (SUNDAY, WEDNESDAY, ETC.)
   X NO GROUPS MINISTRY

4-3. *Which stage, if any, best describes where you are now in your groups ministry?*

   ☐ Stage one—debut          ☐ Stage two—definition
   ☐ Stage three—diversity    ☐ Stage four—decline
   ☐ Other (please specify):

   ☒ No stage. We currently don't have any groups ministry; but at this point, to get
   started, stage ___2___ is our beginning preference.

4-4. *As best you can determine, which category best describes the programmatic phi-losophy in which the small-groups ministry must fit?* (Check one.)

   ☐ Total competition    ☐ Competitive
   ☒ Cooperative          ☐ Total cooperation
   ☒ Other (please specify): SEMI-COOPERATIVE TO START

   ☐ I don't know at this point, but I plan to do the following to find out:

4-5. *How much supervision do the "top" leaders want to provide for the groups ministry?* (Check one.)

   ☐ Complete supervision    ☒ Some supervision
   ☐ Minimal supervision     ☐ No supervision
   ☐ Other (please specify):

   ☐ I don't know at this point, but I plan to do the following to find out:

   How did you arrive at your answer to this question? (Briefly explain.)
   TALKED WITH THE PASTORS AND ELDERS

4-6. *Which category best describes the level of structure your groups ministry must adopt?* (Check one.)

☐ Highly structured ☒ Moderately structured
☐ Minimally structured ☐ Not structured
☐ Other (please specify):

☐ I don't know at this point, but I plan to do the following to find out:

How did you arrive at your answer to this question? (Briefly explain.)
DISCUSSION WITH PLANNING TEAM MEMBERS AND PASTOR

4-7. *What is your church's ministry style?* (Briefly describe.)
STRONG ELDER BOARD

4-8. *The groups ministry you're planning is designed for what level of application?* (Check one.)

☒ A churchwide program
☐ A specific segment within the church (specifically describe or identify):

How did you arrive at your answer to this question? (Briefly explain.)
ELDERS' DECISION

4-9. *Which groups-ministry "path" best fits your groups ministry?*

☒ A "main-path" groups ministry
☐ A "specialty-path" groups ministry
☐ Include both, main path *and* specialty path
☐ Other (please specify):

How did you arrive at your answer to this question? (Briefly explain.)
DISCUSSION WITH PASTOR AND ELDERS

4-10. *Do you plan to link your groups ministry with other adult programming elements in the church?*

☐ Yes, the goal is to develop a linked system.
☒ No, a linked system is not being planned.

How did you arrive at your answer to this question? (Briefly explain.)
DISCUSSION WITH PASTOR AND ELDERS

# STEP FOUR WORKSHEET: DETERMINING MINISTRY "FIT"

Church Name: _____    Date: _____

4-1. *The person filling out this worksheet:*

Name: _____

4-2. *Which classification best describes your church when it comes to its small-groups orientation?* (Check one.)

☐ Traditional church   ☐ Transitional church   ☐ Transformational church

Briefly explain your reasons for checking this category:

4-3. *Which stage, if any, best describes where you are now in your groups ministry?*

☐ Stage one—debut        ☐ Stage two—definition
☐ Stage three—diversity  ☐ Stage four—decline
☐ Other (please specify):

☐ No stage. We currently don't have any groups ministry; but at this point, to get started, stage _____ is our beginning preference.

4-4. *As best you can determine, which category best describes the programmatic philosophy in which the small-groups ministry must fit?* (Check one.)

☐ Total competition   ☐ Competitive
☐ Cooperative         ☐ Total cooperation
☐ Other (please specify):

☐ I don't know at this point, but I plan to do the following to find out:

4-5. *How much supervision do the "top" leaders want to provide for the groups ministry?* (Check one.)

☐ Complete supervision  ☐ Some supervision
☐ Minimal supervision   ☐ No supervision
☐ Other (please specify):

☐ I don't know at this point, but I plan to do the following to find out:

How did you arrive at your answer to this question? (Briefly explain.)

4-6. *Which category best describes the level of structure your groups ministry must adopt?* (Check one.)

☐ Highly structured      ☐ Moderately structured
☐ Minimally structured     ☐ Not structured
☐ Other (please specify):

☐ I don't know at this point, but I plan to do the following to find out:

How did you arrive at your answer to this question? (Briefly explain.)

4-7. *What is your church's ministry style?* (Briefly describe.)

4-8. *The groups ministry you're planning is designed for what level of application?* (Check one.)

☐ A churchwide program
☐ A specific segment within the church (specifically describe or identify):

How did you arrive at your answer to this question? (Briefly explain.)

4-9. *Which groups-ministry "path" best fits your groups ministry?*

☐ A "main-path" groups ministry
☐ A "specialty-path" groups ministry
☐ Include both, main path *and* specialty path
☐ Other (please specify):

How did you arrive at your answer to this question? (Briefly explain.)

4-10. *Do you plan to link your groups ministry with other adult programming elements in the church?*

☐ Yes, the goal is to develop a linked system.
☐ No, a linked system is not being planned.

How did you arrive at your answer to this question? (Briefly explain.)

STEP FIVE
# IDENTIFYING NEEDS AND GOALS

*The way of a fool is right in his own eyes,*
*But a wise man is he who listens to counsel.*
PROVERBS 12:15

**OVERVIEW**—This step is designed to assist you in:

1. Identifying needs as the basis for developing groups-ministry goals.

2. Determining need-assessment levels and methods.

3. Selecting needs for translation into ministry goals.

4. Writing achievable groups-ministry goals.

**B**ack in step 1, during the preplanning phase, you identified various goals to guide the planning process. Based on your planning authority (step 2; also see step 4), your understanding of your context (step 3), and your knowledge of how small groups fit into your church (step 4), now it's time to identify specific goals to guide your groups ministry. Goals are important. If you're not sure where you're headed, you're not likely to get there.

Step 5 is related to step 3—both seek information on which to base your planning. In fact, step 5 logically fits back in step 3, a context audit. Separate or together, both steps are needed. While a context audit is far more general in nature, here in step 5 our efforts are more focused. It's time to pursue a singular aim: to discover specific needs (including interests) in your church that become the basis for developing goals, which in turn guide your small-groups ministry.

Don't skip this step! While a context audit is optional, step 5 is essential. Goals provide paths to follow, targets to aim at, and ends to achieve.

Before attempting to discover the specific needs existing in your church, let me introduce you to some basic biblical goals that serve as bench marks—essential criteria to guide your attempts at equipping your church members to glorify God (1 Corinthians 10:31) and reach our world for Jesus Christ (Acts 1:8).

All small groups in the local church—regardless of their specific purpose or type—share four general, basic goals. In reality, these are *shared goals*. They represent ideals every Christian needs to pursue. Consequently, everything a local church does for its adult members should in some manner seek to attain one or more of these goals. So, it's wise to keep the following basic goals in mind as you begin to explore specific needs and interests within your church:

1. *Nurture biblical love* (see John 13:35; 1 Corinthians 13:13; Galatians 5:13; Ephesians 5:2; 1 John 4:7,11,21)—The Bible is clear: God is love. This divine characteristic isn't an option, it must characterize everyone who claims to be a Christian. However, merely knowing or talking about love isn't sufficient. Biblical love is demonstrated love.
2. *Facilitate unity and* koinonia (see Acts 4:32; Romans 12:5; 1 Corinthians 12:12,14,25; Ephesians 4:3,5,13; 1 John 1:3,6-7)—A genuine, healthy "fellowship" or community of believers is marked by unity (but not necessarily uniformity). Our "oneness" reflects the fact that God is one.
3. *Build the Body* (see Romans 14:19; Ephesians 2:19-22; 4:11-16; Colossians 1:10-12,28; 2:6-7)—Whether the task is to evangelize the lost or disciple believers, the goal is to present all men and women complete (mature) in Christ.
4. *Cultivate spiritual gifts* (see Romans 12:6-8, 1 Corinthians 12:4-11)—Ministry is a mutual, shared task. Every believer shares in the responsibility. Therefore, each Christian must discover and exercise his or her spiritual gift or gifts.

---

*Note:* Later in step 6 you select one or more types of small groups to utilize in your small-groups ministry. This selection process is directly affected by the needs and/or interests you identify at this point and translate into goals. This vital, sequential relationship flow is depicted as follows:

Needs➤Goals➤Type of Groups

---

## IDENTIFYING NEEDS—A NEEDS ASSESSMENT

To get started in developing group-ministry goals, you must first identify the real needs that currently exist among your church's regular adult participants. The following statement guides this "needs-assessment" process:

A needs assessment is conducted in order to identify and select current real needs suitable for translation into goals, which in turn guide the small-groups ministry.

Let's examine several ideas expressed in the above statement. First, the focus is on *current real needs*. For our purposes, a need is an existing requirement, want, lack, or interest; is factual; and is capable of being met now or in the near future in a group context. In other words, a current real need is an actual necessity that presently exists and can be resolved in a small group. Ideally, real needs are affirmed by more than one person. This mutual agreement is important. An individual may have personal needs motivating his or her desire to join a small group, but in a groups ministry the needs must be shared if the group is to succeed.

Second, since you now understand what you're looking for—needs—next you must *identify and select* those needs. The identification process constitutes the heart of a needs assessment and, as we shall see, utilizes various methodologies. Selection comes after the needs are identified. Usually more needs are identified than you can possibly deal with in a groups ministry. Some needs aren't even suitable for consideration. For example, a small group isn't the best way to meet someone's need for improved performance at work, to earn a college degree, or to pay more attention to his or her children. So as you can see, not every need can or must be selected, only those that the planning team thinks can realistically fit into and guide your groups ministry.

Third is the idea expressed in the word *goals*. Goals are our targets; they provide direction for the groups ministry. Goals express needs, and needs are the raw materials upon which goals are built.

But what is a goal? Are goals different from objectives or aims? Do I need all three: goals, objectives, and aims? Some argue that all three types of statements are required. In certain contexts (formal education, ministry training in the local church, etc.), I agree. But in planning a small-groups ministry, identifying needs and formulating goals are enough. Goals and aims are useful tools for planning and conducting individual group meetings.

Our focus is on goals, but definitions for goals, objectives, and aims are presented below:

---

### GOALS, OBJECTIVES, AIMS: WHAT'S THE DIFFERENCE?

*Goals*—General statements in broad terms specifying purposes and/or desired outcomes for the group. One or more goals can be identified and provide direction or purpose for a small group.

> *Example:* Group members will "care for one another" (1 Corinthians 12:25).

*Objectives*—Precise statements identifying (1) knowledge, (2) attitude, or (3) behavior expected as a result of participating in the group, that when demonstrated suggest the complete or partial attainment of its related goal. One or more objectives can be associated with each goal.

> *Example:* After the group has met for three months, group members will begin to assist one another in dealing with spiritual and personal difficulties.

*Aims*—Explicit statements of process, method, and/or steps necessary to accomplish a particular objective within one or more group sessions. One or more aims can be associated with each objective.

> *Example:* Conduct a twenty-minute discussion ("brainstorm" ideas) on how group members can demonstrate caring attitudes and actions toward one another.

---

Fourth, the phrase *"suitable for translation"* refers to the process whereby identified and selected needs are used as the basis for determining and writing goals. Note that I say "writing goals." Written goal statements are the best—they become tangible records and are more easily discussed, adopted, and monitored. We discuss what's involved in the translation process a little later.

## NEEDS-ASSESSMENT GENERAL CRITERIA

It's time to examine the actual processes used to identify needs suitable for translation into goals. Some general criteria may prove helpful in guiding your efforts. So as you begin to think about and prepare to identify your church's needs related to small groups, keep in mind that a successful needs assessment reflects the following characteristics:

*SPECIFIC*—Only ask for and get needed information. It's very easy to lose focus and seek interesting but nonproductive information. For example, asking your adult members when they were baptized is interesting and important information, but not normally necessary for planning small groups.

*OTHER-CENTERED*—The intent is to discover needs among the adult members, not champion personal bias or interests. Therefore, seek to discover and build upon the needs, ideas, and situations of the people you want to serve through the groups ministry.

*UNBIASED*—Traditional standards for objectivity must guide the needs assessment process. Avoid personal or planning team hunches, feelings, or prejudices, as well as unconventional needs assessment methods.

*COLLABORATIVE*—The best needs assessments are team efforts. Assessments are more quickly planned, completed, understood, and utilized when the process is shared.

*SYSTEMATIC*—A well-organized, well-prepared, and well-executed needs assessment is mandatory. Do it right . . . the first time!

*REALISTIC*—A practical, doable needs assessment fits into ministry priorities and available resources (time, people, money). Procedural breadth and complexity must be appropriate to the church's size.

*INFORMATIVE*—A needs assessment, if done right, helps alert your adult members to the benefits associated with small groups. A well-done assessment is an excellent promotional opportunity.

## NEEDS-ASSESSMENT LEVELS, STRATEGIES, AND METHODS

A productive needs assessment, first, must be aimed at a specific target segment within the church—that is, the *level* of application within your church. Small-group ministries are flexible and can be planned to include the entire church—all the adult members—or some recognized suborganization such as all the adult-education classes, or even one individual class. Furthermore, the groups ministry, and the required needs assessment, can include just men, just women, or one particular age group (young adults, college students, etc.). Identifying the assessment level must reflect your answer to this question: "For whom are you planning the groups ministry?" Your answer, subsequently, affects how extensive the assessment must be and whom you need to ask to participate in the needs-gathering process.

Second, to grasp the "how to's" associated with determining needs, it's helpful to identify four different needs-assessment *strategies* and their associated *methods*:

*NONFORMAL*—Unfortunately, this is the most common type of needs assessment. The method is simple: do little or nothing. At best the planning team just "prescribes" the needs or interests it thinks exist among the potential adult participants. Often such prescriptions are based on the team's own personal attitudes, opinions, or ideas. The planning team doesn't talk with anyone, and no attempt is made to confirm the team's conclusions.

*INFORMAL*—In an attempt to avoid a nonformal approach, an informal needs assessment is frequently utilized, even though it isn't the best option. Beginning with some basis—such as the previously stated biblical goals or the team's own ideas on what needs exist (see "Generic Needs and Interests" later in this step)—the planning team members seek to conduct informal conversations with various church members or regular attenders.

Unfortunately, team members often speak only with their friends or relatives who attend the church. Little or no effort is put into assuring a "representative" sample of opinions.

*SEMIFORMAL*—Combining informal and quasi-formal methods is perhaps the *best* approach. Informal personal discussions are combined with "focus groups" (small groups of individuals who are invited to discuss the issues), simple questionnaires, or telephone interviews. Some effort is put into seeking opinions and feedback from the various groups and individuals in the church. The example provided at the end of this step is a semiformal needs assessment (see the "Step Five Worksheet" example).

*FORMAL*—Rarely used by churches, a formal needs assessment utilizes random samples, formal questionnaires, interviews, and rigorous statistical data analysis. Most churches do not have anyone on their pastoral staff trained in formal needs assessment. A layperson in your church may, on occasion, have the necessary training and background. A formal needs assessment, however, usually isn't necessary. Consequently, formal methods are not discussed in this handbook.

## NEEDS-ASSESSMENT QUESTIONS TO ASK YOURSELF
The following questions serve as an outline to help you think about and plan your needs assessment (as always, tailor the process/questions to suit your specific situation):

1. *What is the focus or level of application?* A needs assessment can focus on one age group, adult-education class, organization, etc., or the whole church in general.
2. *What needs information does the assessment seek?* A needs assessment can seek to confirm predetermined potential needs (see "Generic Needs and Interests" later in this step) or allow the assessment participants to report on what they think are theirs or other people's needs (an "open-ended" approach).
3. *Who will the planning team ask to participate?* A wise planning team includes, other than themselves, as wide a span of participants as possible (within the assessment's level of application). Sometimes church records and files are also helpful in identifying needs. For example, if attendance records indicate visitors stay two or three months and then leave, it may indicate the need for a small-groups-assimilation strategy.
4. *What resources are required?* Costs, even if minimal, are involved. A needs assessment takes time, some money, and some materials (paper, copies, postage, etc.).
5. *What method or methods will be used?* There is more than one method to accomplish a needs assessment. The planning team must decide how or by what means it will accomplish the assessment (using a survey, interviews, focus groups, etc.; all the options are not presented in this handbook).
6. *When will the assessment be conducted?* A functional matter—dates and times for doing the assessment must be planned and implemented.
7. *How will the identified needs be summarized or "interpreted"?* Once the needs assessment is completed, you must organize the collected "data" into usable statements expressing needs. This task involves summarizing many statements into fewer representative statements, or if you asked the respondents to rank statements you provided, to tally the results. Note that it's very helpful to

answer this last question early on so you can develop assessment methods that obtain usable feedback.

One additional two-part question accompanies each of the above questions: Who is responsible to do it and by when? This question puts "legs" on the assessment process.

## GENERIC NEEDS AND INTERESTS

Over the years certain *generic needs* have emerged based on people's needs and the dynamics found in many churches. While the list isn't exhaustive, here are a few examples (do you have any additional suggestions?):

- Christian fellowship—Enjoying the company of and interaction with believers.
- Mutual caring—Empathizing with and meeting one another's needs.
- Applied Bible study—Focusing on applied biblical truth.
- "Serious" Bible study—Digging deep into God's Word.
- Mutual prayer—Praying for one another.
- Evangelism—Joining others in a strategy for sharing the gospel.
- Assimilation—Helping new people fit in and become part of the church body.
- Ministry—Doing a specific task or ongoing ministry with a team of people.
- Productive leisure time—Playing with a purpose.
- Accountability—Holding one another accountable to God.
- Encouragement—Seeking to uplift one another's spiritual and emotional health.
- Support—Standing by one another in difficult, trying circumstances.

## TRANSLATING NEEDS INTO GOALS

Translating identified needs into appropriate goals, which in turn provide purpose and direction for your small-groups ministry, is both an art and a science. The "science" part involves definable steps I'll share with you in just a moment. Conversely, the "art" dimension involves making decisions and choices appropriate to your situation. Describing the procedural steps it takes to translate needs into goals (the science) is far easier than trying to explain the many options you face in making appropriate decisions suitable to your situation (the art).

### Selecting Needs for Translation into Goals

Which needs should you select and translate into goals? It's up to you—I can't tell you. This is the "art" in a needs assessment I mentioned a bit ago. You and the planning team must decide which needs you want to address. While it's ultimately your call, let me suggest several things to guide your artistic selections. In general, try to select needs that . . .

- *can be met in a small group.* As mentioned previously, not all needs are suited to small-group ministries.
- *are widely shared or supported.* If the needs assessment reveals that more than 50 percent (or whatever percentage you select) of the respondents/participants think something is a need, you're fairly safe in selecting that need for translation into a goal.
- *fit into your church's ministry "style."* Every church has a ministry style, the type

of ministry the church is known for. Some churches are evangelistic, some are known for their teaching ministries, others have the reputation for social peace and justice, still others focus on helping those who are down and out. Select needs that best reflect your church's style. The "fit" concept is explained more fully back in step 4.

- *you think you can accomplish.* If your church is small and has limited resources (people, time, money), then avoid selecting too many needs or needs that are beyond your abilities. Go slowly at first. Select needs that are realistically doable at this point in your church's life. Expand your groups ministry by building on small, progressive successes.
- *you want to accomplish.* It finally comes down to what you want to achieve through a groups ministry. Whether you want to pursue pressing spiritual issues in your church or merely endeavor to facilitate social relationships, it's your choice.

Let me remind you: Selecting needs for translation into goals is an art, and not everyone has the same taste in art. You'll never please everyone. So do what you believe is pleasing to God!

## Criteria for Goals
Our focus in this step is on goals. Objectives and aims are determined at the individual group level. That is, each group—working as a group—determines how it will achieve its goals (in some cases groups also establish their own goals). Perhaps you can think of others, but here are three useful guidelines to consider as you develop your groups-ministry goals:

MAKE THEM OWNABLE—Group leaders and participants need to "buy" the goals as their own; they must see the advantage the goals offer to themselves and others.

MAKE THEM ATTAINABLE—There is no use in adopting goals so lofty that they're beyond human ability to achieve. On the flip side of the coin, goals that provide no challenge are useless. "Attainable" means reachable by most group members given adequate time.

MAKE THEM MEASURABLE—Similar to objectives and aims, but in more general terms, goals must identify conditions that when obtained are demonstrated in the group members' knowledge, attitudes, and behavior. Simply put, "measurable" means you can see, touch, or experience the identified ideal condition or concept (yes, even "faith" can be demonstrated) cited in the goal.

## Translating Needs into Goals: A Two-Stage Process
Let's assume you've already completed the necessary needs assessment and selected the three needs (an arbitrary number; use as many as you can realistically justify) listed below as the ones you want to translate into goals. These needs are:

1. *Mutual prayer*—Praying for one another.
2. *Accountability*—Holding one another accountable to God.
3. *Encouragement*—Seeking to uplift one another's spiritual and personal lives.

Translating these needs into goals involves a two-stage process:

*STAGE ONE: WRITING THE GOAL STATEMENT.* Here again, writing "acceptable" goals is an art. There isn't one way to do it. Nevertheless, given the selected needs, an understanding of their logical meanings, and the goal criteria (see the previous section, "Criteria for Goals"), I like to write goals with an introductory statement leading the reader to expect the goal statements. The introductory clause should end with the word *to* (but it's not necessary to use the word *goals* in the introductory clause unless you want to). An example follows:

Our small-groups ministry here at Christ Community Church is designed to help active group members to:

1. Pray for one another.
2. Hold one another accountable to God.
3. Encourage one another in their spiritual and personal lives.

*Note:* To accomplish these goals, they were later linked to specific objectives and aims established by the individual groups. However, some churches elect to develop, based on preestablished goals, consistent objectives and aims all groups are required to pursue. This latter condition reflects a "high-control" situation (see step 5).

*STAGE TWO: EVALUATION REVIEW.* Ask yourself these questions: (1) Does the goal statement reflect the selected need's true essence or meaning? (2) Does the goal statement make common sense (not unduly abstract)? and (3) Are the previously discussed criteria for goals met? If you can answer all three questions "yes," you have an adequate goal statement. Congratulations. If not, go back and figure out how to adjust the statement so you can answer the questions in the affirmative.

## A NEEDS ASSESSMENT: ONE EXAMPLE

The worksheet example that follows presents one way to conduct a workable needs assessment. It's a good, middle-of-the-road, *semiformal* alternative. However, many variations are possible and acceptable.

Remember, there is no one right way to do a needs assessment. Make whatever adjustments and use whatever methods are relevant to the planning needs in your situation. After all, the most important thing is to obtain current real needs suitable for translating into goals, which in turn provide purpose and direction for your groups ministry. Methods aren't nearly as important as good results. Therefore, use whatever valid methods you know and understand to accomplish your needs assessment.

# SMALL-GROUPS NEEDS ASSESSMENT

Under the Elders' direction, a Small-Groups Planning Team is exploring the possibility of starting a small groups ministry here at Main Street. Working together, the Elders, Pastors, and Planning Team members identified the following items as possible needs that exist in our church. Please help us by giving us your opinion. Your responses are confidential. Please do not put your name on this questionnaire.

*Instructions:* Based on the needs you think can be met in small groups, which of the following items are among the top five(5) needs present in our church? Please rank the needs you select from 1 to 5; with 1 being the most pressing need, 2 the next most important, and so on.

*Ranking  Potential Need*

_____  **Accountability**—Holding one another accountable to God.

_____  **Assimilation**—Helping new people fit in and feel welcome.

_____  **Bible study**—Life-related, systematic study of God's Word.

_____  **Evangelism**—Joining others in a strategy for sharing the gospel.

_____  **Fellowship**—Being and interacting with other believers.

_____  **Ministry**—Doing a specific task or ongoing ministry with a team of people.

_____  **Mutual caring**—Assisting one another in our spiritual growth and life issues.

_____  **Prayer**—Praying for one another in a regular, systematic manner.

_____  **Recreation**—Productive leisure time activities.

_____  **Scripture memorization**—Committing God's Word to memory.

_____  **Support**—Standing by one another in difficult, trying circumstances.

_____  **Other** (please specify):

Which category best describes your status? (Check one.)

1 _____  Member
2 _____  Regular attender
3 _____  Other (please specify):

Which category best describes your age group? (Check one.)

1 _____  18 to 29 years old
2 _____  30 to 49 years old
3 _____  50 or older

**Thank you!** Your participation is greatly appreciated. PLEASE return this questionnaire by placing it in the box marked "Small-Groups Needs Survey" located on the reception counter in the church lobby.

# STEP FIVE WORKSHEET: IDENTIFYING NEEDS AND GOALS

Church Name: MAIN STREET CHURCH                    Date: _____

5-1. *The person filling out this worksheet:*

Name: DON SWAN

5-2. *What is the needs-assessment focus or level of application?* (One adult class, an age group, etc., or the whole church?)

THE WHOLE CHURCH . . . ALL ADULT MEMBERS—
WE WANT TO ATTEMPT TO HAVE ALL OUR ADULT
MEMBERS CONSIDER BEING IN A SMALL GROUP

5-3. *What needs information does the assessment seek* (confirm needs or an "open-ended" approach)?

X CONFIRMING NEEDS IS THE PRIMARY APPROACH
X ALLOW FOR SOME "OPEN ENDED"

5-4. *Who will the planning team ask to participate in the needs assessment?*

—PASTORS (ODEN AND GLEASON) } HELP IDENTIFY POTENTIAL NEEDS
—ELDERS
—ADULT MEMBERS } CONFIRM IDENTIFIED NEEDS
—CHURCH RECORDS

5-5. *What resources does the needs assessment require?*

—APPROXIMATELY $25-30 TO REPRODUCE THE NEEDS
  SURVEY QUESTIONNAIRE
—PLANNING TEAM'S TIME (E. SWAN AND HOWE ARE SURVEY-
                        ING NEEDS AMONG THE ADULT
                        MEMBERS)

5-6. *What method or methods will be used to conduct the needs assessment?*
(1) NEEDS "BRAINSTORMING" WITH THE PASTORS, ELDERS, AND
    AMONG THE PLANNING TEAM MEMBERS
(2) DEVELOP A SURVEY QUESTIONNIARE TO HAVE ADULTS CON-
    FIRM THE IDENTIFIED NEEDS (COPY ATTACHED)
(3) PLANNING TEAM WILL TALLY THE RESULTS, DEVISE RECOM-
    MENDED GOALS, AND SEEK THE ELDERS' APPROVAL

5-7. *When will the assessment be done?*

    X  PASS OUT THE QUESTIONNAIRE ON TWO SUNDAY MORNINGS
        (JUNE 5 AND 12) IN ADULT ED CLASSES
    X  PASS OUT THE QUESTIONNAIRE AT THE END OF THE JUNE 12
        MORNING SERVICE

    IN BOTH CASES, ASK THE ADULTS TO COMPLETE THE SURVEY
    AND RETURN IT BEFORE LEAVING

5-8. *How will the identified needs be summarized and "interpreted"?*

    —TALLY THE RESPONSES, THE ONES RECEIVING THE HIGHEST
      CONFIRMATION WILL BE SELECTED AS POSSIBLE GOALS
    —IF MORE THAN 30% OF THE RESPONDENTS CITE THE SAME

5-9. *Having completed the needs assessment, what needs are selected to serve as the basis for goals?*

    —THE SURVEY WAS COMPLETED ON THE DATES NOTED;
      211 COMPLETED QUESTIONNAIRES WERE RETURNED

    TOP FIVE:  1-FELLOWSHIP
              2-MUTUAL CARING
              3-PRAYER
              4-BIBLE STUDY
              5-MINISTRY

5-10. *What goals serve as the purpose/direction for your groups ministry?*

    SMALL GROUPS AT THE MAIN STREET CHURCH PROVIDE THE
    OPPORTUNITY FOR PARTICIPANTS TO:

    1. ENJOY THE FELLOWSHIP OF FELLOW CHRISTIANS;
    2. PARTICIPATE IN LEARNING TO CARE FOR ONE ANOTHER AS
       BROTHERS AND SISTERS IN CHRIST;
    3. PRAY FOR ONE ANOTHER ON A REGULAR AND SYSTEMATIC
       BASIS;
    4. STUDY AND APPLY GOD'S WORD; AND
    5. COMPLETE VARIOUS PROJECTS DESIGNED TO SERVE OTHER
       MEMBERS OF OUR CHURCH.

# STEP FIVE WORKSHEET: IDENTIFYING NEEDS AND GOALS

Church Name: _____  Date: _____

5-1. *The person filling out this worksheet:*

Name: _____

5-2. *What is the needs-assessment focus or level of application?* (One adult class, an age group, etc., or the whole church?)

5-3. *What needs information does the assessment seek* (confirm needs or an "open-ended" approach)*?*

5-4. *Who will the planning team ask to participate in the needs assessment?*

5-5. *What resources does the needs assessment require?*

5-6. *What method or methods will be used to conduct the needs assessment?*

5-7. *When will the assessment be done?*

5-8. *How will the identified needs be summarized and "interpreted"?*

5-9. *Having completed the needs assessment, what needs are selected to serve as the basis for goals?*

5-10. *What goals serve as the purpose/direction for your groups ministry?*

STEP SIX

# SELECTING SMALL-GROUP TYPES

**OVERVIEW**—This step is designed to assist you in:

1. Defining "small group."
2. Clarifying the differences between the various group options.
3. Deciding what type of group or groups best fits your situation.

*The plan of the heart belongs to man,*
*But the answer of the tongue is from the LORD.*
PROVERBS 16:1

**A**re all small-group ministries the same? Are there different types or kinds of groups to select from in planning a small-groups ministry? On what basis do I select the type of group to use?

Good questions. This step is designed to help provide answers.

Please note, all small groups are *not* the same. Like people, groups are different. There are different types or kinds of groups designed to accomplish different purposes. Furthermore, even groups in the same category are different. Each group has its own personality and characteristics. It's helpful to sort through and clarify these issues as you plan your groups ministry.

In this step, you must decide what type of group—or groups—you'll include in your groups ministry. To help you do this, we will first define our term *small group*. Then, we must explore the basic types of small groups. Lastly, we'll consider how to select from among the various types.

### DEFINING "SMALL GROUP"

Up to this point we talked about small groups without actually defining the term and concept. So, without further ado, here is my generic definition, the definition we'll use from this point on:

> *A small group within the church is a voluntary, intentional gathering of from three to twelve people regularly meeting together with the shared goal of mutual Christian edification and fellowship.*

A lot is packed into this definition. So, let's examine it phrase by phrase:

*WITHIN THE CHURCH*—Our definition, and this whole book, focuses on groups within the local church. This distinction is important because small groups are used in many other contexts: education, business, military, etc. This makes sense. Small groups are an excellent method to facilitate human interaction and accomplishment. However, groups within the church, unlike most other groups, have a defined spiritual dimension and purpose to their existence. As such, they exist and operate under the direction of the Holy Spirit, utilizing biblical values and standards.

*VOLUNTARY*—People cannot and must not be forced to join a small group. Potential group members must choose to participate. Of course, it can be argued that group membership is a spiritual obligation or duty, but this arm-twisting technique doesn't produce long-term participation. People need to know and understand, see and experience the value of group membership. Just as salvation cannot be forced on people, group attendance must not be forced.

*INTENTIONAL GATHERING*—Small groups are premeditated, planned gatherings of people. They aren't random happenings left to chance. Clear purpose and design characterize the types of groups included in our definition. They systematically bring people together for deliberate reasons.

*FROM THREE TO TWELVE PEOPLE*—Group size is very important! When group membership expands beyond twelve people, it becomes increasingly difficult to maintain effective interpersonal relationships and accomplish the group's goals. This doesn't mean larger small groups won't work, but the likelihood of their success is reduced in proportion to their increased size. I'm reminded that Jesus' group included only twelve people besides Himself. If a group this size was adequate for Jesus, who was God, we're wise to follow His example. Group size comes up again in step 7. So, let's move on.

*REGULARLY MEETING TOGETHER*—Groups can exist on paper only and never meet. Such groups fall outside our definition. We are concerned with groups who gather together on a consistent and frequent basis. Meetings are scheduled for a specific length of time, on an exact day, at a definite time and place. My preference is one and a half hours, on a weeknight, 7:00 to 8:30 p.m., in my or another group member's home. But there are other options we'll explore later.

*WITH THE SHARED GOAL*—The group's purpose or intent is not a hidden secret, for me to know and you to find out. Members participating in groups that fit within this definition understand, accept, and actively promote common goals. The general purpose for the group's existence is openly acknowledged and approved by the group leader and members alike. While many specific goals and objectives may guide a group's existence, two broad ideas are included in our definition. Read on.

*MUTUAL*—The familiar saying "one for all and all for one" captures the "mutual" idea in our definition. Every group member must actively accept the responsibility for the group's success. No idle observers are permitted, only active participants. Members must view their involvement as a blend of both giving to and receiving from the group. Both the leader and members are accountable for group relationships, process, tasks, and goals. This common responsibility is focused on two broad areas, discussed next.

*CHRISTIAN EDIFICATION*—The Greek words for "edify" (*oikodomeo*) and "edification" (*oikodome*) literally mean to "build" or "building up." Add the word *Christian* and the meaning focuses on the idea of strengthening or reinforcing the spiritual lives of believers. Therefore, regardless of the group's specific purpose or activities—evangelism, Bible study, prayer, sharing, etc.—everything must be aimed at building up Christians. This standard was established by the Apostle Paul. In talking about what the Corinthian church did when they assembled together, he instructed, "Let all things be done for edification" (1 Corinthians 14:26).

*FELLOWSHIP*—Our definition recognizes *koinonia* (fellowship) as the dynamic that builds and holds a small group together. More than merely coffee and donuts, biblical fellowship means sharing things in common, communion with one another as an expression of our relationship with Jesus Christ (1 Corinthians 1:9). One of the early Church's key characteristics was fellowship (Acts 2:42). In 1 John 1:7, we are told that if "we walk in the light," we have fellowship with one another. Small groups provide a key context in which we can actively realize genuine Christian relationships.

Numerous different types, models, or small-group applications can fit into our definition. *There is no one right kind or type of group.* Consequently, most church-related groups fit within our definition. Speaking of group types, it's time to examine the options.

## KINDS OF GROUPS

In step 5, you identified the goals to provide purpose and direction for your groups ministry. Now it's time to put those goals to work. Different goals require different groups. As I already said, not all groups are the same. Each group has a central thrust or *primary focus*, the *central reason* for which the group exists: its goals. My experience has led me to identify four basic kinds of groups, all of which fit into our generic small-group definition:

### Relationship-Oriented Groups

A group in this category focuses on being a group. That is, the group's primary focus is on the spiritual and/or social relationships among its members. What the group does—its meeting format—is a secondary issue. Emphasis is placed on group identity, relationship dynamics, and the processes necessary to bring these about. Terms such as "growth group," "caring group," "fellowship group," or "covenant group" are often used to describe groups that fit into this classification.

> *Key Characteristics*
> ✓ Relationships are the key focus.
> ✓ "Process" has priority over content.
> ✓ Heavy emphasis on group dynamics.
> ✓ Many formats or applications are possible.
> ✓ A common "main-path" option (see step 4).

Relationship-oriented groups come in different shapes and forms depending on what format, methods, and activities are used. Here are three examples:

> *ASSIMILATION GROUPS*—To help visitors and new members fit into the church identity and fellowship.
> *GROWTH GROUPS*—To assist Christians in developing their spiritual lives.
> *RECREATIONAL GROUPS*—To facilitate spending leisure time in a purposeful manner.

## Content-Oriented Groups

This second classification includes a variety of Bible study and discussion groups. The main reason for meeting is to study or discuss a biblical passage or topic. Interpersonal relationships are of concern, but normally are merely assumed. Little if any time is spent on dealing with group dynamics. The primary focus is on the content.

*Key Characteristics*
✓ The focus is on information, ideas, and/or intellectual data.
✓ Relationships are important, but at best a secondary concern.
✓ Becoming a group—group development—isn't usually discussed.
✓ Many formats or applications are possible.
✓ A common "main-path" option (see step 5).

Similar to relationship-oriented groups, content-oriented groups also come in various forms. Many applications are possible. Here are two examples:

BIBLE STUDIES—To systematically study God's Word.
DISCUSSION GROUPS—To provide a forum for discussing relevant issues.

## Task-Oriented Groups

These are "doing" groups. The primary thrust is to accomplish a defined task, job, assignment, etc., the group's members do together. Consequently, the group's task, its purpose for meeting, is the reason for the group's existence. Relationships among the members take a secondary role and usually aren't discussed unless a problem arises. The group members may not even view themselves as being a group. Most committees and planning groups fit into this category. Likewise, evangelism groups are usually task-oriented.

*Key Characteristics*
✓ Group shares a defined task.
✓ Relationships are important, but at best a secondary concern.
✓ Members may or may not see themselves as a group.
✓ Multiple formats are possible.
✓ A common "specialty-path" option (see step 5).
✓ Especially effective as "ministry" groups within a local church.

Once again, task-oriented groups come in various forms or applications. From among the numerous options, here are three good examples:

LEADERSHIP GROUPS—To motivate, equip, and encourage individuals who fit into a designated leadership category.
SERVICE GROUPS—To cooperatively accomplish a designated ministry (youth ministry, home and foreign missions, nursing home, rescue mission, etc.).
ADVOCACY GROUPS—To undertake a cause and champion its outcome (pro-life, Bible distribution, antidrug, family life, etc.).

## Need-Oriented Groups

The primary reason underlying this group category is a common need among the group members. Often called support groups or recovery groups, these groups comprise members meeting together for common support and understanding. The group member's attitudes and actions say, "I understand your struggle; I've been there myself." Alcohol recovery, parents of gay children, divorce recovery, or battered women are all examples of need-oriented groups.

### Key Characteristics
✓ Focus is on meeting people's specific interpersonal and intrapersonal needs.
✓ Supporting relationships are important.
✓ Multiple formats or applications are possible.
✓ A common "specialty-path" option (see step 4).
✓ Especially effective as "outreach" ministries to the community.

Many people, many needs. The options for need-oriented groups are endless. Here are four basic alternatives (can you think of others?):

RECOVERY GROUPS—To assist people in maintaining their recovery from addictive habits and/or lifestyles (Alcoholics Anonymous, codependency, overeating, sexual addiction, drugs, etc.).

SUPPORT GROUPS—To assist persons who have suffered significant difficulties in their lives (divorce, cancer, losing a spouse or family member, rape, job loss, etc.).

SELF-HELP GROUPS—To aid people in developing healthy spiritual, psychological, and social habits and/or skills (spiritual disciplines, public speaking, assertiveness training).

GROUP COUNSELING—To deal with personal issues that require the guidance of a professionally trained group facilitator (severe cases of those issues named above).

✶ ✶ ✶

It's useful to keep these four group categories in mind. However, these categories aren't rigid and don't necessarily account for every variation. In fact, there is a trend among some churches to combine several group types and produce hybrid groups. For example, one church in Indiana I'm familiar with is structured around ministry teams, relationship-oriented groups that share a specific ministry task: missions team, junior high ministry team, worship team, etc. It's a great idea that's working well.

Remember, no one type of group is ideal or preferred. All serve a purpose and can be effective. Some churches elect to use only one type, such as relationship- or content-oriented groups, but then utilize various formats and activities within that group type. Other churches, especially larger churches, utilize all four types and even create new options. It all depends on what you're trying to accomplish in or with your groups ministry.

## SELECTING A GROUP TYPE
There is no magic in selecting which type of group to develop your groups ministry around. *It's your choice.* What do you want to accomplish? What needs are represented in your church and what type of group—or groups—is best suited to meeting these needs? In short, the type of group you need depends on the goals you selected back in step 5. If there is any trick to this process, it's having enough information to make wise, informed decisions. If you skipped step 5, good luck in making your decisions. You'll need it.

The following checklist is designed to help you think through the type or types of groups that best fit your situation. Add or subtract from the checklist in any way you think necessary.

### Selecting an Appropriate Type of Group:
### A Checklist

_____ 1. The type of group (or groups) is suitable to the identified needs and goals (refer to step 5).

_____ 2. Supervision requirements are achievable (refer to "Supervision and Structure" in step 4).

_____ 3. The selected type of group is appropriate to the amount of structure desired in the groups ministry (refer to "Supervision and Structure" in step 4).

_____ 4. The type of group fits your church's ministry style (refer to "Church Style" in step 4).

_____ 5. Given the selected level of application (see "Application Levels" in step 4), the chosen type of groups is workable.

_____ 6. The type of group selected fits into and supports the selected groups-ministry path (*main path* or *specialty path*; see step 4).

_____ 7. The type of group chosen is suitable to link (or not to link) with other adult ministries (see "To Link or Not to Link" in step 4).

_____ 8. The planning team agrees on what type of group is needed.

_____ 9. The top leadership accepts the planning team's opinion on what type of group is needed.

_____ 10. The proposed type of group does not seriously compete or interfere with other ministries to which the church is already committed (see "Competition or Cooperation" in step 4).

_____ 11. The potential leadership (assuming some recruiting and training is necessary) is available to lead the type of group selected.

_____ 12. The type of group selected will "sell" to the potential adult group members in our church.

# STEP SIX WORKSHEET: SELECTING SMALL-GROUP TYPES

Church Name: _MAIN STREET CHURCH_ Date: _____

6-1. *The person filling out this worksheet:*

Name: _ELAINE SWAN_

6-2. *Does the "small group" definition provided in this handbook suit your church's needs?*

☒ Yes
☐ No. If no, please define "small group" in a manner appropriate to your situation:

6-3. *What type of group do you plan to utilize in your groups ministry?* (Identify or describe.)

Main Path: TO START

Specialty Path:

Why did you select this type of group? (Briefly explain your reasoning.)
X WE FEEL IT IS THE BEST METHOD TO START A SMALL-GROUPS MINISTRY IN OUR CHURCH
X ELDERS FELT IT WAS THE BEST APPROACH AT THIS POINT IN OUR CHURCH'S LIFE

6-4. *Do you plan to link the groups to other adult ministries?*

☒ No    NOT AT THIS TIME, REEXAMINE THIS ISSUE IN ONE YEAR
☐ Yes, please describe how:

# STEP SIX WORKSHEET: SELECTING SMALL-GROUP TYPES

Church Name: _____ Date: _____

6-1. *The person filling out this worksheet:*

Name: _____

6-2. *Does the "small group" definition provided in this handbook suit your church's needs?*

☐ Yes
☐ No. If no, please define "small group" in a manner appropriate to your situation:

6-3. *What type of group do you plan to utilize in your groups ministry?* (Identify or describe.)

Main Path:

Specialty Path:

Why did you select this type of group? (Briefly explain your reasoning.)

6-4. *Do you plan to link the groups to other adult ministries?*

☐ No
☐ Yes, please describe how:

# NAILING DOWN ORGANIZATIONAL SPECIFICS

**OVERVIEW**—This step is designed to assist you in:

1. Identifying the organizational specifics associated with a groups ministry.

2. Reviewing the many organizational options from which to select.

3. Selecting the specific organizational details appropriate to your church.

*Commit your works to the LORD,*
*And your plans will be established.*
PROVERBS 16:3

**I**t's time to turn our attention to the necessary organizational details associated with building a small-groups ministry. Are you prepared to face this large task?

Here in step 7 you must make decisions in fifteen different areas. Fifteen organizational specifics are a lot to deal with, but they represent most of the functional decisions associated with a groups ministry—they're the nitty-gritty.

A quick reminder of two things before we start: First, there aren't right answers to the various organizational decisions you and/or the planning team face, just appropriate or inappropriate alternatives in light of your situation and your groups-ministry goals. Second, steps 1 through 6 provided you with the necessary background data specific to your situation. Be sure to incorporate this information into your decisionmaking process. Ready? Go for it!

## S1—Groups Size

*How many members in a group?* Groups are collections of individuals. As such, group members often possess divergent opinions, ideas, experiences, attitudes, and expectations. The larger the groups, the more member-related variables your leaders must deal with. Consequently, group success is directly related to group size.

A consensus exists among small-group experts: The ideal group size is between three and fifteen people. Yet, my experience causes me to recommend twelve members as the maximum ideal group size. This isn't a magic number, but it is the figure Jesus selected. It makes sense. If you increase size beyond twelve, you're expanding the number of potential relationships within the group that must be formulated and maintained. Let me explain. As group size increases, the potential interpersonal relationships expand geometrically. A group of twelve members has the potential for sixty-six different relationship combinations.

Increasing the group size by just three persons, to fifteen, results in 105 relationships. So, as you can tell, it's wise to keep "small" groups small.

It's too easy for members to hide in larger groups. I don't mean hide in a physical sense, but in a spiritual, social, or emotional sense. It's much easier for the quiet member to remain silent, the verbal member to dominate, the less committed member to find excuses for not attending, and the fringe member to remain on the periphery. Of course, these liabilities are manageable, but my point is, "large" small groups often present major roadblocks that hinder group development and effectiveness.

In general, limiting your groups to approximately twelve people is the best way to avoid many obstacles and increase the probability to succeed. But this group size is an ideal. Larger groups *can* work if you're willing to put in extra time and effort encouraging the group's communication and relationships.

Please note, the group's type and purpose directly affect group size. I've already argued for limiting groups to twelve members, but some groups—albeit very few—actually work at an acceptable level with larger numbers. Content-oriented groups, for example, are often larger than other types of groups. Conversely, task-oriented groups often work better if they are smaller in number. You are free to disregard the suggestions, but here are *my* group-size recommendations given group type:

| IDEAL GROUP-SIZE GUIDELINES | |
| --- | --- |
| TYPE OF GROUP | RECOMMENDED GROUP SIZE |
| Relationship-oriented Groups | 3 to 15; a limit of 12 is ideal |
| Content-oriented Groups | 3 to 30; a limit of 15 is ideal |
| Task-oriented Groups | 3 to 15; a limit of 6 to 8 is ideal |
| Need-oriented Groups | 3 to 20; a limit of 12 is ideal |

## S2—Groups Membership

*Is group membership cross-generational or from approximately the same age group?* The debate rages: Should groups be homogeneous (same age, social status, etc.) or heterogeneous (mixed ages, social status, etc.)? Good logic and reasoning exist on both sides of the issue. Both approaches work. But which is better? I prefer homogeneous groups in terms of age; *other factors can be heterogeneous* (male or female, rich or poor, educated or uneducated, black or white, etc.). However, please recognize that most people prefer and gravitate to groups in which the members are more like themselves—"birds of a feather fly together." You may not like this fact, but it's the truth, especially in relationship-oriented groups.

My bias toward structuring groups based on members' ages comes from having experienced many approaches. People who are approximately the same age (a five- to ten-year spread) have more in common. This commonality promotes closer friendships, more spiritual growth, and quicker group development. Of course, this logic assumes the groups in question are not task-oriented groups, which do work reasonably well with a cross-generational membership.

Small groups that include mixed age levels are workable, but normally the groups take longer to develop, experience reduced communication, and struggle with the wide diversity of needs present among the members. Nevertheless, many churches elect to structure their entire groups ministry around cross-generational groups. The benefits associated with such a grouping strategy are considered more important than any potential liabilities. Cross-generational groups are especially common in small churches where the number of people within the various age groups is not sufficient to warrant "age-graded" groups.

In addition to the question about ages, what about including children in your groups? In general, I discourage this practice for three reasons: (1) Most children below ten to twelve years of age do not possess the personal and social skills necessary to become "fully functioning" group members; (2) the diversity between a child's and an adult's attention span, spiritual maturity, and educational preferences is too wide for most groups to manage successfully over time (but it can work for three or four meetings); and (3) parents are easily distracted when their children, especially very small children, are present. Adults don't attend their children's Sunday school classes; why should children attend their parents' small group? Groups are for adults. Some individuals are upset by this conclusion and feel strongly that groups should be "family units." So be it, but it's a *very* difficult alternative to make work over the long run. We'll address child care a little later (see S12).

Small groups can be productive ministry tools with junior and senior high school students. Most groups with junior-high, freshmen, and sophomore students require some level of adult supervision, especially junior-high groups. However, by the time students are juniors and seniors in high school, they can participate successfully in self-led small groups because they have the emerging spiritual, personal, and social skills necessary to make a group work.

## S3—Groups Availability

*Is group membership open or "closed"?* Some groups have a fixed or stable membership, while others are intentionally open and accept members at any time. Both approaches have their strengths and weaknesses. Fixed (closed) groups are better for developing long-term, intimate relationships but can become exclusive. Open groups work well in quickly assimilating people but often don't provide the stable relationships conducive to intimate sharing and caring. Content-oriented groups, such as most Bible studies, lend themselves to a "y'all come" approach. On the other hand, groups that stress relationships and are primarily process-oriented need to have fixed memberships. Jesus' group, the apostles, was a closed group. One good exception to this principle is the need-oriented groups—support or recovery groups—which are designed to focus on a specific need. In these situations an open, cross-generational group strategy is often preferred and works best.

When dealing with relationship groups, I prefer fixed memberships. The group remains open during the first four to six weeks, to allow for normal membership adjustments, then closes and remains together for a stipulated amount of time. At the end of the agreed-to time, the group reopens, some members leave, perhaps new members are added, the group recovenants (see S13), and after four to six weeks closes. If included as an element in the groups ministry, this process goes on and repeats itself usually on a yearly basis. This strategy can work for most types of groups.

A church or organization need not limit itself to only one kind of group. With careful planning, it may be desirable to have some groups with open memberships and some where the membership is fixed. Likewise, going back to an earlier issue, some groups may be age-graded while others are cross-generational. The larger a church, the more it becomes necessary to provide a diversity within its groups ministry.

### S4—Groups Formation

*How are groups formed?* How creative are you? There are many, many ways to form groups. However, the specific method used is usually based on one of four general methods: choice, assignment, random assignment, or "find your own."

Allowing people to participate in a group of their choice is my preferred method in forming groups. It spawns an "I want to be in this group" attitude from the start. Adults prefer choices. The best application of this method I've seen was where the group leaders, formats, times, and locations were posted and the church members were then asked to select the group that best fit their schedule and/or preferences. When a group reached twelve members, it was closed. New groups were offered at stated times throughout the year. "Choice" methods in forming groups have merit because they provide options and are easily adaptable to the needs found in most churches.

Some churches and organizations simply assign people to groups. This strategy permits more precision in managing group size and functions. One large church I'm familiar with, which recently changed the practice, used to interview each person and then assign him or her to a group. Careful attention was given to having the right "mix" of individuals within each group. New groups began as needed. A highly structured method that emphasizes control, it's a good alternative in churches with "high-authority" top leadership that wants to closely supervise the groups ministry. Yet, it's often perceived as being heavy-handed and lacking the element of choice most adults prefer.

The third option is to form groups using some means of random assignment. Persons who want to be in a group fill out a short "ballot" stating basic information (name, address, telephone) and place it in a "hat" (some type of receptacle). The total number of participants is divided by ten or twelve to determine the number of groups needed. Names are then randomly drawn and assigned to a group until all the groups are filled. This option works well in situations where the people already know each other and are open to being in any group—situations such as adult-education classes or choirs. It's a workable strategy. But while I've never seen it used to form groups within an entire church, there's no reason to think it couldn't work in smaller churches.

The final general method is to have each leader recruit his or her own group members. A group begins when the leader has gathered a sufficient number of people. One variation on this approach is to have the leaders meet and "divide up" the individuals who expressed interest in joining a group. Another alternative—to assure the whole church is included—is to assign an adult segment to each leader and then restrict their recruiting to that specific classification (i.e., recruit members only among young marrieds, senior adults, or new members, etc.). But whatever strategy is used to implement this "find your own" option, you need to recognize that this method lacks control and may cause a competitive atmosphere among the leaders as they vie for group members.

Select or devise a method suitable to your goals and situation. If the method doesn't work well the first time, you're free to change it next time around. But regardless of the specific method you choose, it's wise to make sure the people in your church feel comfortable with it. This advice is especially true for small churches.

## S5—Groups Life Cycle

*How long should a group remain a group?* There is no required length of time the members must remain together as a group. Here again the options are plentiful and depend on your goals and situation. Most groups exist for a fixed amount of time, from a few weeks to several years. Avoid groups with unstated time limits. Many people feel uncomfortable with—and consequently will not participate in—groups that lack clearly defined time parameters (and expectations).

My preference is to have groups meet for one year—actually most groups meet for eleven months, taking the month of August off. This strategy translates into about forty-five to forty-eight sessions if holidays and other reasons for not meeting are factored in. Taking August off is a concession I don't really like. It is comparable to closing down the worship services during August. But that's another issue.

Given the various goals and objectives pursued by different groups, longer than a year or shorter than a year may be appropriate. One southern California church I'm familiar with uses small groups to assimilate new members. These initial groups only meet for six weeks, then the people are invited to join a more traditional group.

In general, I feel strongly that if groups, especially relationship-oriented groups, are to succeed they must meet for no less than one and a half hours each week for one year at minimum. But this is an ideal. Content- or task-oriented groups often meet only for the length of time it takes to cover the content or complete the task. Need-oriented groups are often ongoing, with membership changing on a regular basis.

## S6—Groups Meeting Frequency

*How often do groups meet?* Ideally, groups meet on a weekly basis. This advice is especially true if you want groups to play a major role in defining (or redefining) your church's ministry style. Weekly meetings communicate the fact that groups play an important role within the overall adult ministry. If a frequency other than weekly is selected, it means extending the time the groups need to "become" groups, meet their intended goals, and contribute to making disciples.

Can groups succeed if they meet less frequently than weekly? Yes, but the definition of "succeed" now even more depends on the groups' goals. Task-oriented groups may not need to meet on a weekly basis. Yet, in my opinion, groups that meet only once per month, or less—especially relationship-oriented and need-oriented groups—are just playing at being groups and don't have much of a chance to succeed. Can you imagine anyone arguing to conduct worship services only once or twice per month? Why, then, does it seem plausible to have groups meet less frequently than weekly? It's only feasible in the minds of those individuals who either don't want small groups or don't understand their role in the church's growth and effectiveness.

Ask yourself, can we meet our desired goals if the groups do not meet on a weekly basis? If you answer yes, how often should they meet—every other week, every three weeks, once a month? It can work, but be prepared to invest more time to reach your goals.

## S7—Groups Meeting Schedule

*When should groups meet?* Do you want to structure the day and time your groups meet, or allow the individual groups to make these decisions? Either option gives you many alternatives from which to choose.

The best days and times are those that assure maximum participation. I've talked with many people who wanted to be in a group but were unable to do so because they had conflicts between their schedules and the group meeting schedule. Some churches get around this potential difficulty by offering groups on different days and times.

If 6:30 a.m. on Monday works, do it. There is no right or perfect day and time. These decisions need to be based on the groups-ministry goals and your people's availability. In general, nights—other than Friday or Saturday evenings—seem to work best for most people.

Some churches elect to have all their groups meet on a specific day and time. While this option has some drawbacks, such as the potential to eliminate people who cannot attend at the specified time, it's attractive in many situations where (1) all the adults are employed in a similar business or industry; (2) a high degree of supervision and structure is desired by the top church leadership; (3) the group meetings have replaced a traditional meeting such as "prayer meeting"; or (4) a quality program is offered at the church for the children, permitting the parents to attend a group.

### S8—Groups Meeting Location

*Where is the best place for groups to meet?* Most groups-ministry experts agree, the ideal location for group meetings is in homes. Private homes provide a relaxed atmosphere conducive to group success—whether the leader's or a member's. Some group ministries encourage groups to rotate among all the members' homes. One caution if you select this alternative: You risk confusion that may lead to poor attendance. If you still want to use a rotation system, I suggest rotating no more than once per month (assuming weekly meetings), and be sure to publish a schedule. If you plan to have your groups meet in homes, here are three important guidelines to keep in mind:

- Be sure everyone knows the location.
- Avoid promoting false expectations on the part of the host/hostess (size of home, elaborate refreshments, etc.).
- Encourage group leaders to have the members help the host/hostess straighten up after the meetings are finished.

Some churches have found it ideal to have groups meet in restaurants. This option works well for early morning breakfasts and lunch meetings with working adults. Many restaurants have private rooms they will let you use if reserved in advance.

On occasion, such as in rural contexts where great distances separate the group members, it may be necessary to have your groups meet in the church building. If this is the case, try to create an informal atmosphere. Set aside a room and furnish it like a living room in a home. In general, do whatever is needed to create an informal, relaxed atmosphere.

### S9—Groups Meeting Length

*How long should each group meeting last?* I recommend no less than one and a half but no more than two hours. Your situation may require more (or less) than this standard. But you'll have the best results if you stick to a maximum two-hour time limit. There are pitfalls associated with longer or shorter meetings (can you think of any others?):

*Pitfalls of Longer Meetings*
- Mental and physical fatigue.
- Easier to waste time.
- Some people drop out or simply choose not to participate.

*Pitfalls of Shorter Meetings*
- Insufficient time to accomplish the agenda, task, purpose, etc.
- A "rushing-it" atmosphere.
- Relationships suffer in favor of "getting on with it."

Encourage your leaders to monitor the time closely. Have them begin and end their sessions promptly at the agreed-upon times. Remind them that their group members' time is their stewardship. Often, even if a group officially ends on time, people don't leave immediately. Those who must go feel free to do so. But as the group becomes a group, many will stick around for a while because they just enjoy being together.

In some circumstances the group members may elect to continue on after the regular stopping time. But this should be a group decision, not the result of just going over time, and not a regular occurrence. I've seen people drop out of groups because they, for whatever reasons, didn't want to or couldn't stay longer than two hours.

## S10—Groups Format and Agenda

The term *format* is used to describe the basic design or structure around which groups are built. *Agenda* refers to the specific activities groups do when they meet, including the exact time sequencing used to facilitate the meetings. At stake are those familiar questions, *what*, *when*, and *who*. Each element is best determined by your particular context and the goals your groups ministry is attempting to achieve. Highly structured group ministries routinely dictate all the answers to format and agenda questions, while less structured ministries allow the individual groups to make some or all of these decisions for themselves.

*What do the groups do when they meet?* This question is harder to answer than it may first appear. The options are numerous. Furthermore, depending on the goals, groups can have many different structures around which the meetings are framed, specific activities are selected, and agendas are developed. Most churches operate their group ministries based on one of the following format structures:

- *Set structure*—Every group is structured the same and does the same thing, following the same predetermined, set agenda.
- *Open structure*—More than one group format is made available, or individual groups can select their own format and agenda.
- *Varying structure*—Groups rotate between several formats and agendas.

An example is needed at this point. Back in 1985, the authors of *Good Things Come in Small Groups* (IVP) recommended a fourfold structure: nurture, worship, community, and mission. Each element is seen as important to group functioning and needs some emphasis each time the group meets. Consequently, specific group activities are planned and agendas are developed around this recommended (or required) format structure.

Let's consider one more example. In discussing his "metachurch" model, Carl F. George (*Prepare Your Church for the Future*, Revell, 1991) suggests a format consisting of what he sees as four essential actions: *love* (pastoral care), *learn* (Bible knowledge), *decide* (internal group administration), and *do* (duties that serve those outside the group). These four components serve as a structural framework—a format (but he doesn't use the term)—for what he calls "cells" or groups. Each cell should include each element, even though the level or mix varies from cell to cell—more of one emphasis, less of others.

Prestructured formats are useful in highly structured group ministries but aren't a necessity. Electing to use one depends on the purpose and goals governing your groups ministry. If it suits your needs, use a structured format to build your agenda; if not, don't.

Keeping in mind your groups-ministry goals, your potential group members, the type of group (relationship, content, task, or need), and any demands a prestructured group format may require, one or more of the following activities may be appropriate for your group meetings:

- Bible study (book or topical)
- Discussion (topic, sermons, etc.)
- Prayer
- Bible study workbooks
- Sharing of personal joys, prayer requests, needs, etc.
- Singing hymns and choruses
- Meditation
- Evangelistic Bible studies
- Casual fun (called "fellowship" by some people)
- A defined task (choir, visitation, leadership board, etc.)
- Bible memorization
- Planning and evaluating group tasks
- Scripture reading
- Films and videos
- Others?

Many more alternatives and/or combinations are possible—only your imagination limits you. But let me mention three things that should influence your choices. First, you may find it preferable to include more than one activity within any given group meeting. Second—this is my favorite option—rotate the activities. One group I was in included personal sharing and prayer in every meeting, but rotated between sermon discussion, focused prayer, and casual fun as our primary group activities. Rotating activities kept the group fresh and dynamic. And last, a specific group agenda isn't an issue if you're going to allow the individual groups to make their own agenda decisions. Rather, your task is to help them sort through and understand the various options as they make their selections based on their goals.

*When to do what?* An agenda is needed to organize the selected group format and activities. You only have so much time to invest in each group meeting—one and a half to two hours. How are you going to organize the time? Are you going to require all groups to use the same fixed agenda, or can they devise their own?

Whatever activities are selected, they must fit into time limits. The common mistake is to include too many activities and run out of time before accomplishing everything planned. To avoid this dilemma, it's helpful to establish time guidelines that stipulate the amount of time allotted to each format segment and activity within one specific meeting. But once again, it all depends on the type of group and the goals. Thinking about relationship-oriented groups, here is one example (assuming the group meets from 7:30 to 9:00 p.m. on a weeknight):

| 7:15-7:30 | Arrive and get a cup of coffee |
| 7:30-7:40 | Welcome, news/reports |
| 7:40-8:30 | Group's main activity (Bible study, discussion, etc.) |
| 8:30-8:50 | Prayer (individually, as a whole group, pairs, etc.) |
| 8:50-9:00 | Administrative details (next meeting, announcements, etc.) |
| 9:00 | Adjourn |

Using a fixed time structure is helpful, but it mustn't become a rope binding creativity or flexibility. It's merely a guideline to help implement a format and structure the group's activities. Nevertheless, it is a good idea to follow the agenda as closely as possible. Being prepared but deciding to deviate from the plan is far better than having no plan and merely wandering about. You must help your group leaders understand these issues and help them strive to become good stewards of their group members' time.

*Who does what?* The group's format and agenda are important, but someone needs to take the responsibility for each activity included in the format and agenda. This is such an important issue I've given the topic its own subsection. Read on.

## S11—Groups Meeting Leadership

*Who leads the meetings?* Assuming the planning team is putting together a groups ministry that includes groups with *designated leaders*—the "official" group leaders—an important question needs answering: Do the designated leaders lead their individual groups every time the groups meet?

Highly structured group ministries, which operate under heavy supervision from the top church leaders, often require their identified leaders to "take charge" and lead all group sessions. It's not uncommon in these situations for the leaders to meet weekly, receive instruction and requirements from a master teacher/leader, and then return to their own groups and teach what they were taught.

Unstructured group ministries, on the other hand, may include groups that do not have designated leaders—leadership is shared by the group members (more in theory than in practice, however). But in most situations the groups included within a groups ministry have designated leaders. The next planning step deals in more detail with structuring and selecting leadership within an entire groups ministry. For now, you should know the alternatives for leading individual group meetings:

- *Identified or designated leader*—This "official" leader is responsible to plan and run all meetings; he or she does every leadership function during the meetings.
- *Rotated among group members*—Only one group member plans and runs a specific meeting, but that individual is different each week. Group members, including the identified leader, rotate the responsibility.
- *Shared leadership*—Working as a team, two or more group members accept the responsibility to plan and run specific group meetings. The needed leadership functions are divided among those sharing the leadership that week, for a number of weeks, or on an ongoing basis.
- *Host/hostess*—The group leader is the person in whose home the group meets that week or month.
- *Combination*—Leading individual group meetings is accomplished by using a mix of the alternatives previously listed.

When all is said and done, here are five principles to keep in mind as you sort out the decision as to who leads the individual group sessions:

✓ Each group session must have a group leader. That leader, whether it's the identified leader or not, must know he or she is responsible to plan and lead the session.
✓ Highly structured group ministries, ones that demand that designated group leaders take charge, require individuals who are more highly trained and skilled, have "status," and are accepted by the group members.
✓ If you decide to rotate the group leadership, avoid forcing people to take a required turn. Some individuals are not willing to assume group leadership, but make fine group members.
✓ Over time, the most successful groups employ some form of rotated and/or shared leadership. It's too easy for group members to become dependent on the skills and leadership of one official leader who leads every session.
✓ Evaluate your selected group-leadership strategy on a regular basis. It may work with some groups and not with others. Furthermore, does the leadership strategy accomplish your goals?

## S12—Child Care

*What do you do with the children?* Are you going to provide child care as part of your groups ministry, or are you going to ask each group to make these arrangements for itself? This is an important question because many parents, especially parents with young children, express their frustration because they want to participate in a group but can't find suitable child care. Are there creative alternatives to resolve this issue? Yes. Here are some I have seen or used:

1. Have the children attend a church-sponsored program designed especially for them (AWANA, Boy or Girl Scouts, Pioneer Clubs, your own creation, etc.). Parents attend their group meetings knowing their children are well cared for. This option demands careful scheduling. Allow adequate time for parents to bring their children, travel to their group meeting, attend the meeting, and then return to pick up their children.

2. Trade off with other groups (or individuals). For example, group A watches group B's kids on Tuesday night while B attends their group, then B watches A's kids on Wednesday evening while A meets.

3. If the groups meet in homes and the particular home in question has a separate large room, one group member, on a rotating basis, cares for the children.

4. Find volunteers or hire one or more sitters to care for the children at the church facility or in a home separate from where any groups are meeting.

5. Include the children; have a group made up of family units. This can work, but be alert to the fact that having children in the group significantly changes the role and potential benefit experienced by the adults.

Every option has its pros and cons. So, before selecting one, don't forget to analyze your specific situation carefully to determine which option best meets your needs.

## S13—Groups Covenant

In my opinion, all group ministries should use group covenants. Does this sound too strong? Perhaps, but covenants are the best tools I've seen to help both the groups ministry as well as the individual groups clarify their purpose, establish goals and objectives, discuss expectations, and define functional issues.

What is a covenant? According to my Funk & Wagnalls, *covenant* is a noun and means: (1) An agreement entered into by two or more persons or parties; a contract. (2) A solemn pledge made by members of a church to maintain the faith, ordinances, etc. (3) The promise of God to bless those who obey him or fulfill some other condition. (4) A written agreement, as a contract, under seal.

The "canned" definition points us in the right direction, but here is a specific definition tailored to small-group ministries you may find useful:

> *A small-group covenant is a written compact or agreement that sets forth specific details, principles, and practices the group members commit themselves to uphold for the specified period of time they meet together as a group.*

*Why should groups have a covenant?* God is our model for using covenants. In the New Testament we read about two covenants—the "old" and the "new"—which govern the relationship between God and man, and between man and his fellow man. It's this biblical precedent and model that sets the stage for small-group "covenanting." Consequently, using a covenant (some people like the term *contract*, but I don't use the word because it means a legal, binding agreement in our culture) can help your groups to do the following:

1. Clarify the purpose for existing and establish its goals.
2. Demonstrate the idea, "You are important to me," because a covenant is in effect a promise or commitment between the members.
3. Clarify the members' expectations.
4. Set the "boundaries" (standards or norms) for group membership.
5. Experience "team building" during the time the covenant is discussed and adopted.
6. Provide a basis for group evaluation.
7. Facilitate change.
8. Communicate group expectations to new members.

*How are covenants developed?* The planning team has two options: to use covenants or not to use covenants. For the sake of discussion, I'm assuming the team sees the merit and decides to use covenants. Subsequently, the team has two more choices: to *stipulate* the covenant all groups use, or to allow each group to *negotiate* its own covenant.

Stipulating a universal covenant works reasonably well in highly structured group ministries. It's quick and helps define the groups ministry and clarifies for potential participants exactly what is expected of them prior to joining a group. But stipulated covenants usually aren't as quickly "owned" by the group members, nor do they permit the group to tailor it to their specific needs. On the reverse side, negotiated covenants frequently take a lot of time to formulate, but permit tailoring and result in higher ownership among the group members.

## AN EXAMPLE OF A "RELATIONAL" GROUP COVENANT

Our small group gives us the opportunity to develop the relationships and fellowship necessary within the Body of Christ. Genuine biblical fellowship *is possible*, with God's help, through our individual and mutual commitment. To assist us as group members in achieving the goals of identification, love, caring, and accountability to God, and to guide us in our mutual commitment to one another as brothers and sisters in Jesus Christ, we agree to abide by the following covenants:

1. *THE COVENANT OF AFFIRMATION AND ACCEPTANCE:* I pledge to accept you. I may not agree with your every attitude or action, but I will attempt to love you as God's child and do all I can to express God's affirming love. I need you; we need each other.

2. *THE COVENANT OF AVAILABILITY:* My resources—time, energy, insight, possessions—are at your disposal if you need them. As part of this availability, I pledge to meet with you in this group on a regular basis.

3. *THE COVENANT OF PRAYER:* I promise to pray for you regularly.

4. *THE COVENANT OF HONESTY:* I agree to strive to become a more open and honest person, to share my true opinions, feelings, struggles, joys, and hurts as well as I am able. I trust you with my dreams and problems.

5. *THE COVENANT OF FEEDBACK:* I pledge to mirror back to you what I am hearing you say and what you are feeling. If this means risking pain for either of us, I trust our relationship enough to take the risk, realizing it is in "speaking the truth in love, we are able grow up in all aspects unto Him, who is the head" (Ephesians 4:15). I will try to express this feedback in a sensitive and controlled manner, in keeping with the circumstances.

6. *THE COVENANT OF SENSITIVITY:* Even as I desire for you to know and understand me, I pledge my sensitivity to you and your needs to the best of my ability. I want to hear you, see your point of view, and understand your feelings.

7. *THE COVENANT OF CONFIDENTIALITY:* I promise never to divulge anything shared within this group in confidence outside this group. I vow not to push you to share things about yourself that you would prefer to keep undisclosed.

In full acceptance of these covenants, I affix my name to this document in recognition of my commitment to God and the members of this group. I shall keep this document as a reminder of this voluntary covenant I've entered into on this date.

_____     _____
Signature                                              Date

(Your signature is for your own commitment; you retain this document.)

*What are some typical covenant "stages"?* If the planning team elects to have each group negotiate its own, the covenanting process usually moves through three stages as the group members seek a mutually acceptable agreement:

PRECOVENANTING STAGE—Talking about the concept, its possibilities and benefits. This usually takes one or two sessions. Be sure to provide the group leaders with biblical and group-dynamics background information.

COVENANTING—The actual process of formulating the covenant may take two to four sessions, depending on the specific group. One alternative to assist the process is to provide a "blank" covenant that outlines the specific choices and options group members may include in their covenant. As well, I routinely provide groups I lead with a "premade" covenant (see example on previous page) to start the discussion. They're told it's on my computer and can be changed in any way they see appropriate. (Refer to page 97.)

EVALUATION AND RECOVENANTING—The covenant serves as an objective basis for group evaluation during the time the group meets (formative evaluation) and when it's time to disband (summative evaluation). If necessary, this evaluation may require retooling the covenant itself or reaffirming the covenant for another period of time.

*What areas or topics are included in a covenant?* Covenants lend themselves to three different approaches: (1) administrative/procedural covenants that outline how the group functions, (2) relationship covenants that stipulate how the group members treat one another, or (3) covenants that include both areas. Depending on the approach you take, you can include some or all items listed below in a covenant:

- Group goals
- Meeting parameters (day, time, place, etc.)
- Length of duration of the group (weeks, months, years)
- Membership—who? open or "fixed"?
- Participation "norms" or expectations
- Confidentiality when it comes to personal sharing
- Meeting format (do what?) and agenda (time structure)
- Child care
- Refreshments/hospitality
- Others?

Group covenants aren't the answer to every difficulty your groups ministry may encounter. However, they're one key factor in assisting the ministry to succeed. Covenants are well worth the time and effort invested by the planning team and your individual groups.

## S14—Starting New Groups

*When and how are new groups started?* Earlier we discussed how to form your initial groups. Now you need to determine when to start the initial groups and when and how to add new groups once the groups ministry is under way. As with all the specific organizational details we've discussed, there are various options for starting and adding new groups. Let's first examine when to start your initial groups, then take a look at when and how to add new groups.

*When to start your initial groups?* The obvious answer to this question is: *when you're ready*. Yet don't be fooled; there's more to it than meets the eye. As you contemplate when to start your initial groups, be sure to observe these guidelines:

- The details discussed in this step must be finalized. "Finalized" means you worked through the issues and have come to tentative decisions, allowing for any necessary adjustments that may be necessary once the groups are under way.
- Group leaders must be recruited and trained. You cannot start groups without the necessary "designated" leaders, leadership leaders, and ministry leaders (see step 11).
- The season must be right—starting in the fall (September or October) is a common alternative. Many churches start their groups around the same time the public schools begin the new academic year.
- Don't rush it! Even if you have to postpone the starting date, avoid kicking off your groups ministry if you're not in compliance with the previous three guidelines.

*When and how do you start new groups?* Once the initial groups ministry begins, at some point you may have to add one or more additional groups (let's hope so!). There are no quick answers, but here are four possible times for adding new groups:

PREDETERMINED STARTING TIMES—Groups start at fixed times during the year. For example, each September and February. Most churches use this option.

WHEN-NEEDED STARTING TIMES—When enough people are ready (you pick a number—six or eight) and a leader is prepared, the group begins. Most people who want to join a group are willing to wait a reasonable period of time before actually joining. The trick is to find out what's reasonable and to help the potential new members understand and be patient with the "when-needed" start-up system.

INTERVAL STARTING TIMES—New groups come "online" every month, six weeks, quarter, etc., without regard for the month, season, or other factors. This option works well for large churches that start many new groups during a given year.

ADD TO EXISTING GROUPS—Rather than starting new groups, add new people to existing groups. This option is a big favorite with many churches. It works for some types of groups such as task-oriented groups and content-oriented groups, and in some cases ongoing need-oriented groups, but I don't recommend it for most kinds of relationship-oriented groups. Adding new people to relationship-oriented groups after the groups have met for four to six weeks causes the loss of whatever trust and confidentiality the members have achieved to that point. In effect, the group must begin all over again because the new members make it a "new" group.

The last option, *add to existing groups*, forces the planning team to deal with an important issue: Do you want your existing individual groups—specifically "main-path" groups (see step 4)—to add new people up to a certain membership size and then divide and form a new group? (Some people don't like the words *divide* or *split* and refer to this process as "birthing" new groups.) This strategy for "growing groups" is nice in theory, but I've rarely seen it work well over the long haul. Most groups—specifically relationship-oriented and need-oriented groups—view the process as "splitting up our group." Asking a group to divide (birth, whatever) and form a new group is very traumatic after the members have formed close bonds.

If this adding/dividing option is selected, its success very much depends on three factors: (1) that the group's purpose and goals lend themselves to the strategy, (2) that the expectation is built into the system from the very beginning, and (3) that everyone knows about it prior to joining the "mother" groups. When it's a planned part of how the groups work, adding/dividing can be an exhilarating experience. Each individual group plans for it, encourages its happening, and then celebrates its accomplishment.

## S15—Groups Resources and Budget

*What resources are needed and available for your groups and groups-ministry leadership?* This question focuses on discovering what published resources are necessary to establish and maintain the groups ministry, its leadership, and the individual groups. Identifying any needed resources provides one basis for developing an initial and ongoing budget. However, in some cases the identified resources may already be available in your church library, at local or national denominational headquarters, or in the library at a local Bible college.

Three kinds of ongoing published resources are usually necessary: (1) group curricula, (2) training materials, and (3) what I call "encouragement resources." Group curricula commonly include books, study guides, and workbooks designed for use in small groups. Training materials include handbooks—such as the one you're now reading—manuals, and books designed for assisting you to train group leaders. Lastly, encouragement resources are books, articles, videos, etc., aimed at providing ongoing encouragement and motivation for groups-ministry leadership at all levels.

As you think about possible resources you may want to use, please ask yourself these questions:

- Do I want to write my own materials or use published materials?
- If published resources are used, how must they be adapted to fit my situation?
- How does the material help in meeting the groups' purpose and goals?
- Are the materials suitable for the intended purpose?
- Are the materials appropriate given my leaders' abilities and backgrounds?
- Is cost a factor in selecting published materials?
- Is everyone expected to use the same materials?
- What methods are used to distribute the materials to my leaders?

*What are your budget needs?* Every church has its own budgetary system and requirements. Be certain to comply with these expected requirements as you put together your groups-ministry budget.

In formulating your budget you can either ask for the exact amount you determine is necessary and then be thankful for whatever amount you get, or you can find out how much you can have and develop a budget around that amount. With either option be as realistic as possible. Some churches play the "budget game": Ask for way more than what you want or need, because everyone knows you'll only get a small fraction of the amount anyway. This game is unproductive and must be avoided.

Formulate a comprehensive budget, one that includes all possible areas that require expenditures. Your situation may demand some additional categories, but listed below are the basic items every small groups ministry budget must include:

- ✓ Administrative items (paper, postage, telephone, etc.)
- ✓ Published resources (books, manuals, workbooks, etc.)
- ✓ Publicity tools (posters, mailings, brochures, etc.)
- ✓ Recruiting and training needs (retreat facilities, refreshments, materials, etc.)

How much do you budget for each item listed above? I can't give you an exact answer; your answers depend on several things: the groups ministry's application level (the whole church, one class, etc.), how many different types of groups you have, the number of individual groups, and your leadership structure. The bigger the groups ministry, the more money it takes.

## PUTTING IT ALL TOGETHER

This step is the most time-consuming, as it involves many detailed issues. As you turn to and begin working with the "Step Seven Worksheet," don't fret. Keep in mind that you and the planning team are making initial, hopefully well-informed decisions that may need revision somewhere down the line. Trust God to give you the necessary wisdom.

MAIN STREET CHURCH
# SMALL-GROUP COVENANT GUIDELINES

Each group is asked to develop a covenant to clarify how they plan to operate during the year they meet together. Formulating your covenant is an important process in becoming a group. Consequently, spend at least one or two group meetings on this vital task. Your group leader is prepared to assist your group in completing this critical process.

Your covenant can take whatever form/layout best suits your group's needs. However, the small-groups ministry team recommends you include the following items in your final covenant:

1. When (day, time) and where the group meets.

2. In addition to the general goals guiding all groups sponsored by Main Street Church, any unique goals your group wants to adopt.

3. Your basic agenda, format, curriculum, etc. What will you do?

4. Attendance expectations.

5. Participation "norms" or expectations.

6. Confidentiality when it comes to personal sharing.

7. How you will deal with visitors and/or new group members.

8. If appropriate, how refreshments/hospitality is handled.

9. If necessary, what you plan to do with your children during the meetings.

10. Other issues you as a group want to include.

Please give two copies of your final covenant to Mr. Don Swan, the elder responsible for small-group ministries. Thank you!

# STEP SEVEN WORKSHEET: ORGANIZATIONAL SPECIFICS

Church Name: _MAIN STREET CHURCH_     Date: _____

7-1. *The person filling out this worksheet:*

Name: _ELAINE SWAN_

7-2. *Ideally, and given the type or types of groups you selected in step 6, what is the maximum number of members you want in your individual groups? (S1)*

12-15 Members in "main-path" groups
N/A Members in "specialty-path" groups

7-3. *Based on your answer to question 7-2 and the number of potential participants in your church, how many groups do you anticipate needing initially to start the groups ministry?*

Between _4_ and _20_ groups (minimum and maximum)
BUT SHOOTING FOR BETWEEN FOUR AND SIX GROUPS THE FIRST YEAR

7-4. *Is group membership based on homogeneous and/or heterogeneous guidelines? (S2)*

☐ Homogeneous, based on (specify selected basis):

☐ Heterogeneous, no limitations or restrictions
☒ Both homogeneous and heterogeneous; please describe:
TWO-HETEROGENEOUS (OPEN TO ANYONE)
FOUR-HOMOGENEOUS (BY AGE GROUPS)

7-5. *Are the groups going to have open or closed memberships? (S3)*

☐ Open membership
☒ Closed (fixed) membership after the _SIXTH_ week
☐ Both open and fixed; please describe:

7-6. *How do you plan to form the groups? (S4) (Describe the method and the supporting logic.)*
SIGN-UPS DURING THE LAST TWO WEEKS OF AUGUST AND FIRST TWO WEEKS OF SEPTEMBER

7-7. *Are the groups open-ended, or is there a definite period of time they remain together as a group? (S5)*

☐ Open-ended, no stipulated length of time
☒ A stipulated period of time; please specify the length: ONE YEAR (11 MONTHS)
☐ Some open-ended and some with stipulated periods of time; please explain:

7-8. *How often do the groups meet?* (S6)

☒ Weekly
☐ Less than weekly; please state the frequency:

☐ A mix, both weekly and less than weekly; please explain:

7-9. *When do the groups meet?* (S7)

☐ On a set day and time; please specify:

☒ On various days and times; please specify: EACH GROUP DECIDES FOR ITSELF

☐ Both set and various days and times; please describe:

7-10. *Where do groups meet?* (S8)

☒ In private homes; specify whose if possible and make the necessary arrangements:
EACH GROUP WILL DECIDE FOR ITSELF

☒ Other than private homes; please explain:

TALK ABOUT HAVING ONE GROUP MEET IN THE CHURCH BUILDING SO OLDER CHURCH MEMBERS AND/OR THOSE WHO LIVE CLOSE HAVE ANOTHER OPTION

7-11. *Ideally, how long does each group meeting last?* (S9)

☒ One to one and a half hours
☐ Other; please specify:

BOTH THE PLANNING TEAM AND ELDERS FEEL STRONGLY ABOUT STAYING WITHIN THE TIME LIMITS . . . . STRESS THIS FACT DURING LEADERSHIP TRAINING.

7-12. *What group format and agenda is planned?* (S10)

☐ A set format and agenda; please describe:

☒ Individual groups are free to develop their own format and agenda; please
describe any guidelines and/or assistance provided to help them do this task:
—DISCUSSED IN LEADERSHIP TRAINING
—DECISIONS ON SPECIFICS MUST SUPPORT GROUP MINISTRY GOALS
☐ A mix, both fixed and group-designed formats and agendas are planned;
please explain (complete both items above):

7-13. *Who leads each group meeting?* (S11)

☐ The designated leaders lead every group meeting.
☐ The meeting leadership is rotated among the groups members; please
describe how it's rotated:

☐ The meeting leadership is shared; please describe how it's shared:

☐ The host/hostess leads the group meeting.
☒ A combination of meeting leadership options is planned; please explain:
EACH GROUP DECIDES FOR ITSELF . . . BUT THE DESIGNATED
LEADER BEGINS THE GROUP BY LEADING THE SESSIONS FOR AT
LEAST THE FIRST 6 WEEKS

7-14. *What do you do with the children?* (S12) (Explain how you will deal with this
issue.)
FOR THE FIRST YEAR, EACH GROUP MUST MAKE THE
NECESSARY ARRANGEMENTS. LORD WILLING, NEXT YEAR WE'LL
DEVELOP A SYSTEMATIC PLAN TO ADDRESS THIS ISSUE

7-15. *Are you going to use a group covenant?* (S13)
☒ Yes, please specify:
☐ A set covenant all groups use (please attach a copy)
☐ Each group develops its own covenant.
☒ Each group develops its own using a provided outline (please attach a
copy of the outline). GIVE EACH GROUP LEADER: (1) A COPY OF
☐ No                                     OUR RELATIONSHIP COVENANT;
(2) A COPY OF OUR GUIDELINES

7-16. *When and how are new groups started?* (S14)

☒ The initial groups start on (specify a date): WEEK OF SEPT 18

☒ New groups start (specify a date):

    ☐ At predetermined times; please specify:

    ☒ When needed; please describe how you determine "when needed":
—WHEN 8-10 PEOPLE ARE READY TO BEGIN A GROUP
—A LEADERSHIP COUPLE IS AVAILABLE

    ☐ At various intervals; please specify:

☐ Add new members to existing groups and "birth" new groups when needed; please describe the criteria for how this works:

7-17. *What resources are needed and available for the groups and groups-ministry leadership?* (S15)

Please determine and then list the resources needed in the following categories (circle the items you can obtain from various sources without purchasing):

Group curricula:
JEFF EDGAR IS GOING TO PLACE IN THE LIBRARY—EACH GROUP MUST PURCHASE ITS OWN MATERIALS

Training materials:
DEB HOWE IS INVESTIGATING THE ALTERNATIVES

Encouragement resources:
EVERY LEADER WILL ACQUIRE A COPY OF HOW TO LEAD SMALL GROUPS (MCBRIDE, NAVPRESS)

7-18. *What is your budget? (S15) Determine and list any budgeting requirements that must be met in developing and submitting the groups-ministry budget:*
THE TREASURER AND ELDERS WANT REALISTIC, APPROXIMATE DOLLAR AMOUNTS . . . DON'T "PAD" THE BUDGET

List the items in the budget, how much is needed, and how the amount was determined:

| ITEM | AMOUNT | RATIONALE |
|---|---|---|
| X    Administration | $50.00 | LONG DISTANCE/ETC. |
| X    Resources | $300.00 | LIBRARY RESOURCES |
| X    Publicity | $210.00 | POSTERS, BROCHURE |
| X    Recruiting and Training | $150.00 | MATERIALS, REFRESHMENTS |
| X 10 COPIES OF HOW | $60.00 (10X$6) | |
|    TO LEAD SMALL GROUPS | | |
|     | $770.00 | FOR THE FIRST YEAR |
|     | | |

7-19. *Do any or all of the details outlined on this worksheet need approval from someone or some group other than the planning team?*

☐ No approval is needed.
☐ Yes, everything must be approved by (specify):

☒ Yes, some of the details must be approved (specify which ones and approved by whom):

☒ S1 — CONSULT WITH PASTORS
☒ S2 — ELDERS
☐ S3
☒ S4 — CONSULT WITH PASTOR ODEN AND ELDERS
☒ S5 —    "     "     "     "     "    '
☒ S6 —    "     "     "     "     "    '
☒ S7 —    "     "     "     "     "    '
☐ S8
☐ S9
☒ S10 — CONSULT WITH ELDERS
☐ S11
☐ S12
☐ S13
☒ S14 — ELDERS
☒ S15 — ELDERS (BUDGET APPROVAL)

# STEP SEVEN WORKSHEET: ORGANIZATIONAL SPECIFICS

Church Name: _____ Date: _____

7-1. *The person filling out this worksheet:*

Name: _____

7-2. *Ideally, and given the type or types of groups you selected in step 6, what is the maximum number of members you want in your individual groups?* (S1)

_____ Members in "main-path" groups
_____ Members in "specialty-path" groups

7-3. *Based on your answer to question 7-2 and the number of potential participants in your church, how many groups do you anticipate needing initially to start the groups ministry?*

Between _____ and _____ groups (minimum and maximum)

7-4. *Is group membership based on homogeneous and/or heterogeneous guidelines?* (S2)

☐ Homogeneous, based on (specify selected basis):

☐ Heterogeneous, no limitations or restrictions
☐ Both homogeneous and heterogeneous; please describe:

7-5. *Are the groups going to have open or closed memberships?* (S3)

☐ Open membership
☐ Closed (fixed) membership after the _____ week
☐ Both open and fixed; please describe:

7-6. *How do you plan to form the groups?* (S4) (Describe the method and the supporting logic.)

7-7. *Are the groups open-ended, or is there a definite period of time they remain together as a group?* (S5)

☐ Open-ended, no stipulated length of time
☐ A stipulated period of time; please specify the length:
☐ Some open-ended and some with stipulated periods of time; please explain:

7-8. *How often do the groups meet?* (S6)

☐ Weekly
☐ Less than weekly; please state the frequency:

☐ A mix, both weekly and less than weekly; please explain:

7-9. *When do the groups meet?* (S7)

☐ On a set day and time; please specify:

☐ On various days and times; please specify:

☐ Both set and various days and times; please describe:

7-10. *Where do groups meet?* (S8)

☐ In private homes; specify whose if possible and make the necessary arrangements:

☐ Other than private homes; please explain:

7-11. *Ideally, how long does each group meeting last?* (S9)

☐ One to one and a half hours
☐ Other; please specify:

7-12. *What group format and agenda is planned?* (S10)

 ☐ A set format and agenda; please describe:

 ☐ Individual groups are free to develop their own format and agenda; please describe any guidelines and/or assistance provided to help them do this task:

 ☐ A mix, both fixed and group-designed formats and agendas are planned; please explain (complete both items above):

7-13. *Who leads each group meeting?* (S11)

 ☐ The designated leaders lead every group meeting.
 ☐ The meeting leadership is rotated among the groups members; please describe how it's rotated:

 ☐ The meeting leadership is shared; please describe how it's shared:

 ☐ The host/hostess leads the group meeting.
 ☐ A combination of meeting leadership options is planned; please explain:

7-14. *What do you do with the children?* (S12) (Explain how you will deal with this issue.)

7-15. *Are you going to use a group covenant?* (S13)
 ☐ Yes, please specify:
　 ☐ A set covenant all groups use (please attach a copy)
　 ☐ Each group develops its own covenant.
　 ☐ Each group develops its own using a provided outline (please attach a copy of the outline).
 ☐ No

7-16. *When and how are new groups started?* (S14)

☐ The initial groups start on (specify a date):

☐ New groups start (specify a date):

☐ At predetermined times; please specify:

☐ When needed; please describe how you determine "when needed":

☐ At various intervals; please specify:

☐ Add new members to existing groups and "birth" new groups when needed; please describe the criteria for how this works:

7-17. *What resources are needed and available for the groups and groups-ministry leadership?* (S15)

Please determine and then list the resources needed in the following categories (circle the items you can obtain from various sources without purchasing):

Group curricula:

Training materials:

Encouragement resources:

7-18. *What is your budget? (S15) Determine and list any budgeting requirements that must be met in developing and submitting the groups-ministry budget:*

List the items in the budget, how much is needed, and how the amount was determined:

| ITEM | AMOUNT | RATIONALE |
|---|---|---|
| ____ Administration | | |
| ____ Resources | | |
| ____ Publicity | | |
| ____ Recruiting and Training | | |
| ____ | | |
| ____ | | |
| ____ | | |
| ____ | | |

7-19. *Do any or all of the details outlined on this worksheet need approval from someone or some group other than the planning team?*

☐ No approval is needed.
☐ Yes, everything must be approved by (specify):

☐ Yes, some of the details must be approved (specify which ones and approved by whom):

☐ S1
☐ S2
☐ S3
☐ S4
☐ S5
☐ S6
☐ S7
☐ S8
☐ S9
☐ S10
☐ S11
☐ S12
☐ S13
☐ S14
☐ S15

# DECIDING ON LEADERSHIP

*Prepare plans by consultation,*
*And make war by wise guidance.*
PROVERBS 20:18

**OVERVIEW**—This step is designed to assist you in:

1. Clarifying the options for leadership levels.

2. Designing an appropriate leadership organization.

3. Deciding on how many leaders are needed at each leadership level.

**Y**ou and the planning team must determine what type and how many leaders are required for your groups ministry. Here in step 8 you decide on the necessary leadership structure or organization, the necessary leaders, and the number needed. Then in step 9 you'll turn your attention to enlisting and training those leaders.

## WHAT LEADERSHIP LEVELS ARE NEEDED?

Starting and running a small-groups ministry is best accomplished by involving as many people in leadership as possible. A collaborative effort, in other words. Okay, but what leadership is needed? While there are many possibilities when considering the potential leaders you'll need to run a successful groups ministry, three primary and essential leadership levels are necessary:

### Groups-Ministry Leaders

These individuals are responsible for the overall groups ministry. They decide how the groups ministry is designed; determine what type of groups are needed; and in general facilitate the *who, what, when, where,* and *why.* Functionally, ministry leaders assume the day-to-day responsibilities associated with overseeing and operating the groups ministry. Usually ministry leaders are laypersons, but in some large churches the pastor or an associate pastor is directly involved.

Ministry leaders may or may not have the authority to decide and act on their own. It all depends on the amount of authority delegated to them by the "ultimate" policy makers, the "top" leaders in your church—usually your pastor and/or the church's governing board. In some cases you may have to deal with authorities outside the church at a denomination, diocese, or association level. Consequently, ministry leaders usually are required to check with and secure the approval of the "bottom-line" policy leaders before implementing decisions that affect the church's philosophy of ministry, scheduling, personnel, or financial resources beyond a certain level.

It's fairly common for some or all of the planning team members to stay to serve as ministry leaders, to form the ongoing groups-ministry team. Of course, this isn't a requirement, nor is it always feasible.

### Leadership Leaders

These leaders lead leaders; they encourage, motivate, assist, and in general help the individual group leaders succeed. Each leadership leader, or whatever you call them (coordinators, facilitators, coaches, etc.), assumes a supervisory-caring relationship with a fixed number of small-group leaders. Leadership leaders may also serve as ministry leaders, giving oversight to the entire small-groups ministry, but it's not a necessity. They're usually laypersons, but here again, in some large churches a pastor may take an active role in leading leaders. This leadership level is an optional role in small churches, but it's especially important in large churches with more than fifteen groups.

### Small-Group Leaders

These individuals provide the critical "front-line" leadership; they lead individual small groups. Small-group leaders are most often laypersons trained for the job. However, in order to set an example and demonstrate how important small groups are in your church, if possible, it's a terrific idea for your pastor to lead a group (important, but not absolutely necessary). In some cases, such as needs-oriented groups, the small group is led by a professional (counselor, psychologist, advisor, etc.) or a semiprofessional (layperson with special training). Note: See the definition for "small-group leader" in my other book, *How to Lead Small Groups* (NavPress, 1990), page 31.

### ORGANIZATIONAL OPTIONS

Given the three basic leadership levels just described, you need to formulate a leadership organizational system that utilizes whichever levels are appropriate and workable in your church situation. Here are three different leadership organizations to consider:

### Organization Option One

This option works best in small churches because it's the simplest. The small-group leaders come together and form the groups-ministry team. These leaders not only lead the overall groups ministry but they also lead specific small groups. The second leadership level, leadership leaders, isn't needed. A pastor may or may not serve on the groups-ministry team in this situation—it depends on how much structure and supervision are desired (refer to step 4).

### Organization Option Two

As a groups ministry grows, the ministry leaders' role and leadership leaders' role often are mixed together but remain distinct from small-group leaders. For example, in one church I attended, the small-groups ministry was led by eight individuals who also served as leadership leaders. This group set whatever policy was necessary for the ministry to run smoothly, and each member also provided supervisory-caring leadership for a specific number of small-group leaders. The leadership group was separate from the elder board, but an elder and an associate pastor were among the eight. When a decision needed board ratification, the elder and/or pastor in the Shepherd Group (groups-ministry team) served as the team's courier and spokesperson to the board, and then communicated the board's decision back to the team. It worked fairly well.

### Organization Option Three

This option is well suited to very large churches. Each leadership level operates in a distinct but interrelated relationship with the others. Ministry leaders oversee the entire groups ministry and supervise leadership leaders. Former group leaders serve as coaches to the individual small-group leaders. The individual small-group leaders then lead specific small groups. What it amounts to is a clear, logical division of labor. Quite frequently a full-time small-groups pastor oversees group ministries in this category.

*Which leadership organizational structure do you need?* As with everything we've discussed, it's your choice. Most churches can operate very successful group ministries using the first or second option. Option three becomes necessary when a church has a very diverse groups ministry and requires numerous well-structured leadership functions to operate smoothly.

### WHAT QUALIFICATIONS MUST THE LEADERS POSSESS?

Before determining what type of leaders you need, and certainly before planning how you're going to enlist and train those leaders (step 9), you must identify the qualifications you are looking for in your potential leaders. Who can serve as a leader? Are there different qualifications for different leadership levels?

Let me suggest FAT people make the best leaders.

**F**aithful (reliable and consistent)
**A**vailable (willing and with adequate time)
**T**eachable (eager to learn)

FAT people come in all sizes and shapes. There is no one personality type, gender, or background that makes a perfect leader. Remember Jesus' apostles—now there was a mixed bag of individuals. Nevertheless, in addition to being FAT, it's a good idea for your leaders also to possess several other characteristics:

*IS NOT A NEW CHRISTIAN (1 TIMOTHY 3:6)*—In nearly all cases, it's best that your leaders are self-proclaimed believers who have at least several years of experience as Christians. The actual length of time varies. After all, some individuals grow quickly in the Lord while others show little progress even after many years.

*DEMONSTRATES AN ACTIVE, GROWING RELATIONSHIP WITH CHRIST (2 PETER 3:18)*—Can you tell the person is a Christian? Do his or her attitudes and actions manifest a relationship with Jesus Christ?

*ENJOYS SERVING PEOPLE (GALATIANS 5:13)*—People who don't enjoy servant leadership shouldn't be asked or coerced into leadership. Group ministries demand people-oriented persons who delight in helping other people.

*HAS A "VISION" FOR SMALL-GROUP MINISTRIES*—The best FAT people, when it comes to small groups, are individuals who have a vision for and are excited about participating in a dynamic ministry modeled after Jesus' earthly ministry, one that has great potential for building the Church.

*HAS EXPERIENCE WITH GROUPS*—Experience with group ministries is very helpful, especially for ministry leaders, but not absolutely essential.

*IS A TEAM PLAYER*—Small-group leaders are part of a ministry team that must rely on each other. Likewise, if leading a specific small group, the leader must see himself or herself as a fellow group member as well as the group's servant-leader.

Can you think of any additional qualifications needed in your context, requirements demanded by your church? Your church may insist that small-group leadership possess one or more of these additional qualifications:

✓ Church membership

✓ Doctrinal agreement

✓ Specific gender (males only?)

✓ Approved by the elders, deacons, etc.

✓ Marital status

I've highlighted various qualifications. Must a person possess all of them in order to serve? No. No one is perfect. Yet, the planning team must sort through and decide which qualifications are required and to what degree. Furthermore, do leaders at all three levels need to meet the same qualifications? Yes. In my thinking, a leader is a leader. Whatever qualifications you and the planning team adopt must be evenly applied across the board, expected of all leaders. Perhaps the only exception to this "rule" in my thinking is the amount of experience with small-group ministries it takes to serve on the groups-ministry team or as a leadership leader, as compared with the experience required for serving as an entry-level small-group leader.

## WHAT ABOUT JOB DESCRIPTIONS?

In my opinion, job descriptions aren't optional, they're essential. Starting with the planning team, everyone involved in the groups ministry needs to accurately understand his or her job. Therefore, well-developed and clearly written job descriptions are indispensable.

Good job descriptions are very practical tools in helping you plan, implement, and run the groups ministry. Precise, *written* descriptions are valuable because they help you:

- Define specific leadership tasks and expectations.
- Identify necessary qualifications for service.
- Specify terms of service.
- Clarify authority relationships.
- Evaluate the leaders' performance and success.

*What goes into a job description?* All leadership levels within the small-groups ministry need job descriptions. Consequently, "good" job descriptions are specific to the task and context (your church's "personality"), thorough and descriptive, and brief and to the point (avoid long, wordy descriptions; one page is usually sufficient). Applying this criteria, I suggest you develop job descriptions which include the following sections:

*POSITION TITLE*—An exact job title contributes a lot to quickly understanding the specific job in question. Titles need not be elaborate or flashy, just descriptive.

*RESPONSIBILITIES*—Describe the specific, exact functions, tasks, and commitments required by the position. It's easy to go overboard and include every tiny detail associated with the job. Avoid this. Merely include the essential, defining tasks—those things they're held accountable to accomplish.

*QUALIFICATIONS*—Outline the exact minimum qualifications a person must possess to serve in the job. Here again, it's very easy to make the list so comprehensive that no mere human could qualify. Include only the key, vital qualifications.

*TERM OF SERVICE*—How long does the position last? Don't overlook this; it's important. People want to know the expected time commitment. This topic is examined more fully a bit later.

*COMMUNICATION LINES*—Identify who will serve as his or her immediate "supervisor" (coach, coordinator, facilitator, etc.)—the individual he or she can go to for assistance or when facing difficulties. Naming a specific person is preferred when possible, but the supervisor's position title is mandatory. In some cases the supervisor isn't a person, but a group. For example, the groups-ministry director is directly responsible to the elder board.

*RESOURCES*—The last section lists all the items available to help the person succeed. Commonly included are things like specific training opportunities, budgets, published resources, or other "benefits." In short, this section describes what you provide the person to help him or her do a good job.

*Who does what?* In step 7 (see S11) we talked about dividing up the responsibilities for leading individual small-group meetings, and earlier in step 2 the various decision-making responsibilities or categories were identified. These two bits of information reflect possible items to include in the "responsibilities" section on the job descriptions. In addition, and depending on your leadership organization, here are some more tasks to divide up according to their possible leadership levels (add, subtract, mix, or match as appropriate for your groups ministry):

### Groups-Ministry Team

✓ Conduct needs assessments.
✓ Write vision statement and ministry goals.
✓ Oversee the small groups' theological/philosophical foundations.
✓ Write job descriptions.
✓ Structure and organize the groups ministry.
✓ Recruit and train group leaders.
✓ Establish and monitor a budget.
✓ Promote and publicize the groups ministry.
✓ Maintain communication with "top" church leadership on groups issues.
✓ Evaluate the groups ministry.

### Leadership Leaders

✓ Maintain communication with small-group leaders.
✓ Encourage small-group leaders.

✓ Assist group leaders to deal with difficult situations.
✓ Assist group leaders with group evaluation.
✓ Collect and review reports and evaluations.
✓ Assist with group membership changes or problems.
✓ Coordinate resources needed by group leaders.
✓ Conduct "in-service" training.
✓ Report group needs to the groups-ministry team.

### Small-Group Leaders

✓ Explain the groups-ministry vision and purpose.
✓ Assist the group in establishing their covenant.
✓ Clarify expectations.
✓ Encourage participation among the members.
✓ Plan and lead group meetings.
✓ Organize and administer functional details.
✓ Attend planning and training opportunities for group leaders.
✓ Maintain communication with a leadership leader.
✓ Recruit possible leaders from among group members.
✓ Model openness and caring.
✓ Facilitate group decisionmaking.
✓ Prepare and submit any required reports.
✓ Evaluate group progress.

## HOW LONG DOES A LEADER SERVE?

"How long do I serve if I accept the position?" is a common response people give when they're asked to assume any volunteer position, including small-group ministries. People need to know not only what they are being asked to do, but also how long you're asking them to do it. The United States is a time-conscious culture.

So how long *do* ministry leaders, leadership leaders, and individual small-group leaders serve? Sorry, no set answers. It depends, as always, on your church situation and groups ministry. In one church it may be a specified period of time, in another the term of service may be open-ended. What works in one church may not work in another. Yet, experience has proven several things:

1. Defining the length of service increases recruiting possibilities. Few people are willing to accept or make an open-ended commitment, especially volunteers. Knowing how long the position lasts assists a candidate in evaluating the opportunity.

2. Terms of service longer than one year aren't a good idea. A person can, and in most cases will (hopefully), renew his or her yearly commitment. One-year terms are ideal because they (1) define time limits most people are willing to accept and

(2) give everyone the opportunity to reassess continuing involvement on a regular cycle.

3. Open-ended or multiple terms of service must be monitored carefully. Even with one-year terms, some people faithfully serve for many consecutive terms. Normally this is very acceptable. However, don't allow a good thing to go haywire because you fail to keep track of who's doing what. Sometimes a person stays in a position far past the point where he or she is effective.

## HOW MANY LEADERS ARE NEEDED?

As you would suspect, the number of leaders you need depends on your groups-ministry level of application, number of individual groups, and any unique demands present in your church. Consequently, I cannot give you exact recommendations, but here are some guidelines to consider:

*GROUPS-MINISTRY TEAM*—The same standards as those for the planning team apply.

| Church Size (Average Adult Participants) | Team Size (Number of Members) |
| --- | --- |
| 50 to 150 | 3 |
| 151 to 500 | 3 to 5 |
| 501 to 1,000 | 5 to 7 |
| 1,001 to 1,500 | 7 to 9 |
| 1,501 to 2,000 | 9 to 11 |
| 2,000 or more | 11 to 13 |

*LEADERSHIP LEADERS*—Approximately one "coach" for every five, but no more than seven, small-group leaders.

*SMALL-GROUP LEADERS*—One trained leader for each small group (apprentice leaders are discussed in step 9).

When determining the number of leaders required, it's never inappropriate to overestimate, especially with small-group leaders. If I know three are needed, recruiting four or five not only meets the goal but allows for adding more groups when needed or filling any leadership voids should an existing or potential leader leave. Even if I end up with too many potential leaders, it's always a smart idea to have them serve as "assistant small-group leaders" for a period of time.

Having assistant or apprentice leaders makes sense. This alternative has two major benefits. First, serving as an assistant leader is a terrific leadership-training method, which we discuss in step 9. Second, it provides an opportunity to see these folks in action prior to their leading their own groups. Then, once they have proven themselves as a small-group leader, they become eligible for serving as leadership leaders and/or for joining the groups-ministry team.

*What about co-leaders or shared group leadership?* Is it possible, at the individual group-leadership level, to fill the "designated leader" role with co-leaders, husband-wife teams, committees or teams of individuals, etc.? Yes, certainly. Some group ministries in fact prefer husband-wife group leaders or some similar shared-leadership alternative. But it isn't an either-or decision. It's quite possible to use both individuals and teams of individuals to serve as designated group leaders. If some form of shared leadership sounds like a live option in your situation, be sure to (1) require all individuals to complete any prerequisite initial and/or ongoing training, (2) not permit one team member to do all the work (husband-wife teams are notorious for the wife doing all the work), and (3) have the leadership leaders monitor the team's communication and cooperation.

# STEP EIGHT WORKSHEET: DECIDING ON LEADERSHIP

Church Name: MAIN STREET CHURCH          Date: _____

8-1. *The person filling out this worksheet:*

Name: DON SWAN _____

8-2. *What leadership levels are needed?* (Check those that are needed.)

☒ Groups-ministry team
☐ Leadership leaders
☒ Small-group leaders
☐ All of the above
☐ Other (please specify):

8-3. *Which leadership organizational structure is best for the groups ministry?*

☐ Option one: Small-group leaders are also the groups-ministry leaders; no leadership leaders.
☒ Option two: Groups-ministry leaders and leadership leaders are the same individuals, but they're different from the small-group leaders.
☐ Option three: Groups-ministry leaders, leadership leaders, and small-group leaders are all different people doing distinct but interrelated ministries.
☐ Other (please specify):

8-4. *What qualifications must individuals at leadership levels possess?* (Please list.)
—CHRISTIANS
—CHURCH MEMBERS
—ATTEND TRAINING
—HAVE THE TIME TO INVEST IN THE MINISTRY

8-5. *What distinct qualifications, if any, are required of individuals at each leadership level?* (Please list.)

Groups-ministry leaders: IDEALLY, PRIOR SMALL-GROUP EXPERIENCE; VISION FOR SMALL GROUPS, TEAM PLAYER

Leadership leaders: (NONE AT THIS POINT)

Small-group leaders: SAME AS LISTED ABOVE IN 8-4

117

8-6. *How long do the individuals serve in the various leadership levels?*

☐ Less than one year; please specify:

☒ One year; specify exact months to begin and finish: GROUP LEADERS— SEPT TO AUG

☒ More than one year; please specify: MINISTRY TEAM WILL HOPEFULLY STAY TOGETHER LONGER THAN ONE YEAR

8-7. *Can some or all leaders serve consecutive terms of ministry?*

☐ No

☒ Yes; please explain specifics: NO LIMITS ON TERMS OF SERVICE; MUTUAL RENEWAL EACH YEAR AFTER INFORMAL PERFOR- MANCE REVIEW

8-8. *Based on the best estimates, how many leaders are needed at each applicable level?*

Groups-ministry leaders: 5    (AT LEAST TO START)

Leadership leaders: 0    (NONE AT THIS POINT)

Small-group leaders: 4-8

Other (please explain):

8-9. *Can individual small-group "designated leaders" be something other than one person (a shared role)?*

☐ No

☒ Yes; please explain: WE WANT COUPLES TO SERVE AS GROUP LEADERS (IDEALLY, BUT NOT A RIGID REQUIREMENT)

# STEP EIGHT WORKSHEET: DECIDING ON LEADERSHIP

Church Name: _____ Date: _____

8-1. *The person filling out this worksheet:*

Name: _____

8-2. *What leadership levels are needed?* (Check those that are needed.)

- ☐ Groups-ministry team
- ☐ Leadership leaders
- ☐ Small-group leaders
- ☐ All of the above
- ☐ Other (please specify):

8-3. *Which leadership organizational structure is best for the groups ministry?*

- ☐ Option one: Small-group leaders are also the groups-ministry leaders; no leadership leaders.
- ☐ Option two: Groups-ministry leaders and leadership leaders are the same individuals, but they're different from the small-group leaders.
- ☐ Option three: Groups-ministry leaders, leadership leaders, and small-group leaders are all different people doing distinct but interrelated ministries.
- ☐ Other (please specify):

8-4. *What qualifications must individuals at leadership levels possess?* (Please list.)

8-5. *What distinct qualifications, if any, are required of individuals at each leadership level?* (Please list.)

Groups-ministry leaders:

Leadership leaders:

Small-group leaders:

8-6. *How long do the individuals serve in the various leadership levels?*

☐ Less than one year; please specify:

☐ One year; specify exact months to begin and finish:

☐ More than one year; please specify:

8-7. *Can some or all leaders serve consecutive terms of ministry?*

☐ No
☐ Yes; please explain specifics:

8-8. *Based on the best estimates, how many leaders are needed at each applicable level?*

Groups-ministry leaders:

Leadership leaders:

Small-group leaders:

Other (please explain):

8-9. *Can individual small-group "designated leaders" be something other than one person (a shared role)?*

☐ No
☐ Yes; please explain:

STEP NINE

# ENLISTING AND TRAINING LEADERS

**OVERVIEW**—This step is designed to assist you in:

1. Determining who is responsible for recruiting and training.

2. Preparing and doing leadership recruiting.

3. Planning for leadership training.

*Without consultation, plans are frustrated,*
*But with many counselors they succeed.*
PROVERBS 15:22

**T**he time has finally arrived to begin recruiting (that is, enlisting) and training the leaders you determined in step 8 to be necessary. Who's responsible to enlist and train is our first topic covered in this step, then we turn our attention to planning the specific recruiting and training activities.

### WHO'S RESPONSIBLE TO RECRUIT AND TRAIN?
*Who's responsible?* The first thing we must do is identify the specific party that is responsible for planning (and later doing) the recruiting and training. These two vital tasks won't get done by themselves. Normally the planning team decides on who is responsible. On occasion, however, the church's official governing board (session, committee, etc.) may want a say in the decision. In other situations an individual, such as the pastor or member of the pastoral staff, is vested with the authority to determine programmatic and personnel issues. But at this point the planning team must clarify who makes the decision and see that it's made.

For the purposes of this handbook, I'll assume two things: (1) The same people aren't responsible for both enlisting and training; these are separate tasks; and (2) the planning team possesses the necessary authority to select the person or persons responsible for both the recruiting and training tasks.

*Is an individual or a committee responsible?* The easiest alternative is to put one individual in charge of recruiting and another in charge of training. This option is a good choice for many small churches. Larger churches may find it more advantageous to have a sub-committee made up of planning team members share the load. Each church situation is different and the options are endless. Here are several basic alternatives from which to choose, all of which work:

1. One person (a planning team member, some layperson other than a team member, an elected church leader, the pastor, or another paid staff member, etc.) works alone.
2. A planning team member is in charge, but enlists other non–team members to form a temporary committee to assist with the task.
3. An elder, pastor, or elected church leader works with a permanent (or temporary) committee of laypersons (which in effect results in the need to recruit recruiters), who are coordinated by the planning team but are not on the planning team.
4. The church pastoral staff works together as a committee.
5. The planning team itself plans both recruiting and training and then assigns the implementation to one or more team members.
6. Members on the planning team divide themselves into two subcommittees, one for recruiting and one for training.
7. Your creative alternative, suitable for use in your church situation.

Selecting the same leadership strategy for both recruiting and training isn't required. The planning team may find it better to use a different leadership structure for each task. In addition, although it's not absolutely necessary, the planning team is wise to develop brief job descriptions for the persons assuming the recruiting and training jobs. This way no one can say, "I didn't know I was supposed to do that."

## RECRUITING

Once the recruiting task is assigned, it's time to go to work planning the process. The recruiters must immediately clarify three things: what to do, who does it, and when it is done.

*What to do?* Recruiting leaders for all levels in the groups ministry is a hard but exciting challenge. Clearly outlining that challenge—the explicit recruiting tasks—is the best way to begin. Listed below are some common tasks associated with enlisting leadership for a small-groups ministry. The list isn't exhaustive, but it gives you a starting point for identifying those tasks appropriate for your church situation:

- Organize the recruiters (if more than one or two persons share the task).
- Plan the recruiting process.
- Identify potential candidates.
- Conduct recruiting interviews.
- If necessary, have leadership candidates approved.
- Maintain recruiting as an ongoing process.

*Who does it?* After determining what to do, it becomes necessary to identify who is responsible for accomplishing the outlined tasks. Three basic options are available:

1. If only one person is responsible for recruiting leaders, he or she doesn't need to worry about dividing the tasks up with anyone else. Yet, in this situation the wise individual finds at least one or two other people to help when additional help or expertise is needed.

2. When recruiting is a shared task (two people, the planning team, a committee, etc.), the chairperson can simply assign specific tasks to each member. Exercise caution when implementing this option. Merely assigning tasks to people doesn't assure a completed job.

3. Another shared-task strategy is to have the members spend their initial meeting identifying what must be done and then dividing the tasks up among themselves. This way the members own their individual tasks and the overall recruiting process. I recommend this option.

A quick question: Are the same people going to recruit leaders for all levels, or will they focus on recruiting leaders only for one leadership level (that is, groups-ministry team, leadership leaders, and small-group leaders)? Sometimes recruiting is a divided task. The planning team, working together, recruits both the small-groups ministry team (or merely takes on that role after the initial planning is completed) and the leadership leaders. Then, specific individuals on the planning team, or a completely different committee, are responsible to recruit small-group leaders. The larger your church, the more you need to consider dividing the recruiting tasks into separate leadership-level recruiting responsibilities.

Whatever method is selected to divide up the recruiting responsibilities, make certain everyone knows who is doing what. It may seem like overkill, but written job descriptions can ward off a lot of misunderstandings. At least write down who is going to do what. Leaving it to memory is risky.

*When is it done?* Putting time limits on the various recruiting tasks and the entire process is often perplexing, but it's a necessity. The best approaches take into account two important issues: (1) how many leaders are needed (see step 8) and (2) any "constraints" that must be accounted for within your church. For example: the requirement to coordinate with a churchwide personnel committee, the necessity to have leadership candidates approved by a higher governing authority, or perhaps the need to complete the recruiting process within certain time limits.

Time is an important factor in successful recruiting. If the new leaders were needed yesterday, not much time exists for recruiting—the situation is urgent. Often, ideal recruiting options are forfeited due to time pressures. In such cases you may be forced to do something or enlist someone you'd rather help find another ministry. On the other hand, if the leaders aren't needed for several months, you have some breathing room.

While there is no fixed, absolute standard for how much time is needed for recruiting, overestimating the required time is far better than underestimating it. It frequently takes six to eight weeks or more—remember, recruiters are volunteer laypersons—to recruit quality persons. And as already mentioned, the number of leaders one must recruit puts constraints on time. It makes perfect sense: The more leaders needed, the more time it takes.

Planning ahead is difficult. Consequently, the ideal strategy is to view recruiting (and training) as an ongoing, never-ending process. This is especially true for large and/or growing churches.

## Recruiting Issues

To assist the recruiters in doing their jobs, it's helpful to consider some important issues associated with recruiting.

*How many potential new leaders are needed?* The answer to this first issue is found in step 8. Remember, the answer must include figures for each leadership level—how many groups-ministry leaders, leadership leaders, and small-group leaders. This previously determined number now becomes a specific objective for the recruiters to accomplish.

*What qualifications must the potential leaders possess?* Review the qualifications you identified in step 8. Remember, these are ideal qualifications. You must determine to what level each candidate reflects the qualifications and if that level is acceptable. Be biblical and realistic, but avoid lofty standards that would prohibit most people from serving.

*What about job descriptions?* Written job descriptions are an essential element in a successful recruiting process! The descriptions were developed during step 8 (do it now if you haven't already), but it's helpful to review their importance. They serve two vital purposes: (1) to clearly delineate job expectations and (2) as a means to explain the potential ministry during the actual recruiting process. In addition, well-written job descriptions provide the basis for evaluating the leaders' performance (see step 12).

*How are potential leaders identified?* One of the most difficult tasks in recruiting potential small-group leaders is identifying qualified candidates. This responsibility requires five considerations:

A GENERAL APPEAL FOR LEADERS, OR A SELECTIVE PROCESS—A pastor I know who serves in a large church routinely makes general appeals from the pulpit and in the church's newsletter, asking people to serve as small-group leaders. Since he needs numerous leaders and the turnover among the current leaders is greater than he likes, he's thrilled to get anyone he can.

While it's a fairly easy method to implement, experience suggests that making general appeals for leaders isn't the best recruiting method in most churches. Yet, it may be acceptable for your church. If so, be sure to heed these guidelines:

1. Uplift the importance of the leader's role; avoid making it sound like a simplistic or unimportant ministry.
2. State the expected leadership requirements; avoid suggesting that leadership in the groups ministry doesn't have standards or make demands.
3. Allow time between appeals; avoid making general appeals so frequently that people routinely expect them and *ignore them*.

Most churches find it preferable to avoid general appeals and implement a selective recruiting methodology that focuses on specific persons. The key here is finding a workable plan appropriate to the particular situation.

When considering selective systems for recruiting leaders, keep in mind three things: (1) Adopt realistic expectations—don't demand or wait for perfect individuals; (2) allow enough time—selective recruiting strategies take more time and effort than general appeals; and (3) plan for the long run—selective strategies work best when implemented over a period of time, when they are an ongoing process, not merely a one-shot attempt.

HOW POTENTIAL LEADERS ARE IDENTIFIED—With ample prayer as a foundation, here are some alternatives for both general appeals and selective recruiting (can you suggest others?) to direct your attempts in identifying potential leaders.

FOR GENERAL APPEALS—

1. Have them fill out a response card (name, address, phone). Ask them to turn it in to someone (an usher, the person making the announcement, etc.) or mail it to the church office. Contact each individual personally within one week after receiving his or her response card.
2. Invite them to attend a potential leaders' information meeting. Stress that their attendance doesn't commit them to serving as a leader; it's just an opportunity

to learn more about the ministry. Hold the meeting in an informal setting such as a private home. Be prepared, be positive, and keep the meeting short and sweet. Seek to arrange a private meeting with each person or couple who attends.

3. If you have regularly scheduled small group leadership training, invite people to participate as "explorers." Be sure they understand that participation doesn't obligate them—it's only an opportunity to get a feel for the small groups ministry. Be sure to follow up these "visitors."

*FOR SELECTIVE RECRUITING—*

1. Ask your present small-group leaders to suggest members in their groups they think would make good leaders. If they don't offer any suggestions, ask them to assist in recruiting by keeping their eyes open to spot future potential leaders.
2. Ask your church lay leaders (elders, deacons, teachers, officers, etc.).
3. Working with a few individuals—perhaps a mix of pastors and lay leaders—identify people who meet the required leadership qualifications.
4. Ask the adult church members and regular attenders for suggestions. To assist them in making their recommendations, publish job descriptions for the various leadership positions in the church newsletter, post a copy on a special bulletin board dedicated to small-group ministries, or include a brief description in the weekly worship folder.

Once your candidate lists are formulated (a separate list for each leadership level is the best idea), spend adequate time praying over the lists. Ask God to prepare the potential candidates for your contact, pray for their responses, and pray for the recruiters as they present and explain the ministry opportunity.

*REQUIRED PREAPPROVAL, IF ANY*—If necessary, secure any approvals necessary to approach the individuals on your prospect list. Some churches have individuals or committees who oversee all recruiting. They serve as a clearinghouse to make sure that all personnel needs are given serious attention and individuals aren't approached by two or three ministries at the same time. Then in other contexts, the pastor or church board must approve contacting anyone being asked to assume a leadership position in the church. In short, find out and secure any "official" approvals needed prior to beginning the actual recruiting interviews.

*THE RECRUITING INTERVIEW*—Don't recruit people in the church halls or parking lots. Contact each candidate individually and arrange an interview.

The best method for making the *initial contact* to set up an interview is a method the recruiter feels comfortable using. Furthermore, it's likely that more than one contact method is needed because each candidate is different. Among the many alternatives, here are three commonly used initial contact strategies:

*THE NATURAL OPPORTUNITY*—Avoid forcing it, but if you already know the person and the opportunity arises during the course of routine interaction, ask to meet with him or her.

*TELEPHONE*—A favorite contact method. Call when you know the prospect is home. Avoid calling him or her at work, around mealtimes, or late at night.

*LETTER AND TELEPHONE*—First send a letter introducing the ministry opportunity, telling the person why you're writing to him or her, and asking for an interview. Explain when you plan to call to schedule a date and time, then follow through.

However the initial contact is made, be sure to (1) explain where you got his or her name, (2) ask for the opportunity to sit down for forty-five minutes to an hour to explain the small-groups ministry and how the person can potentially fit in, and (3) determine a mutually agreeable time and place to meet. If during the initial contact the prospect expresses no interest, thank him or her for the time and conclude by asking the person to pray for you as you seek God's direction in finding the right leaders for the small-groups ministry.

For those who agree to an interview, be sure to keep the appointment (and don't be late). How the interview is conducted communicates a tremendous amount to the prospect about the small-groups ministry's nature and importance, as well as his or her potential involvement. Consequently, the wise recruiter or interviewer makes certain the following interview guidelines are operative:

1. Be friendly and open. Help the person feel relaxed. Quickly review the purpose for meeting (for example, "I'm excited about discussing your potential leadership role in our small-groups ministry") and state how long the meeting will last (forty-five minutes to an hour—don't go overtime!).
2. At minimum, make certain to cover the criteria used in selecting potential groups-ministry leaders, explain the specific role and tasks you want the person to consider, review the job description, and answer any questions he or she may have.
3. In closing the interview it's important to (1) reinforce the idea that it's a spiritual decision and you want to give the person time to pray about it before deciding (encourage married candidates to discuss the issue with their spouse); (2) state the amount of time he or she has to consider the ministry, plus clarify when and how the person will be contacted (phone, letter, in person) for a decision; (3) tell the recruit how to contact you if further questions arise; and (4) conclude with prayer and thank the recruit for the time.

*REQUIRED POSTAPPROVAL, IF ANY*—Whether or not a preapproval was needed prior to conducting the recruiting interview, often a final approval is required afterward to officially recognize a person's leadership role. Here again, the approving individual or group must "sign off" on the person's eligibility based on spiritual and/or other qualifications (see step 8). Once the candidates have said yes (or no—praise the Lord anyway) and any needed approval is secured, the next requirement is to provide them with initial training so they can begin their ministries.

## TRAINING

Planning for leadership training should start about the same time the recruiting planning begins. Then once the recruiting task is completed, or at least well under way and nearing the point where sufficient numbers of new leaders are recruited, it's appropriate to start thinking about beginning to offer the leadership training. But back in the initial planning phases, the trainers must clarify the same three issues the recruiters had to: what to do, who does it, and when it is done.

*What to do?* Most church situations lend themselves to two training systems: preservice training and in-service training. Interestingly, most churches understand the preservice training concept. In-service training, unfortunately, doesn't share the same recognition level. Yet, you need to understand and offer both systems.

Preservice training is a sort of ministry "boot camp." It is initial training designed to (1) impart the church's small-groups vision by explaining how groups fit into church life and ministry; (2) equip the recruits with essential group-leadership knowledge and skills; (3) describe the administrative details associated with how groups operate in your church; and (4) launch them into leadership with the desire to serve and the confidence to begin.

In-service training, on the other hand, comes later. Once the groups-ministry leaders are actively involved, their "teachability" is increased and they're usually eager for more training. Ongoing training then is designed to expand leadership skills, provide knowledge on small-group theory, encourage and boost morale, and maintain open communication lines.

Both preservice and in-service training lend themselves to many different training models. No one model is ideal. So it becomes necessary for churches to select a model or models—more than one is often needed, especially in large churches—that suit their exact needs and they can successfully accomplish.

Back in 1990, while serving as a writer and trainer for Serendipity, I identified seven models being used to train people for various leadership levels in small-group ministries. Today, the models are still being used effectively. Can you think of other models besides these seven?

*CLASS*—A leadership course involving multiple classroom sessions offered over several weeks or months; can include multiple trainers/teachers; fits all leadership levels; works best when adequate time exists prior to starting small groups and/or as an integral element in an ongoing groups ministry.

*PILOT (MODEL) GROUP*—Experience-based training in a group context; "watch-then-do-it" approach with feedback and encouragement; an ideal training model, especially for small-group leaders; excellent method for pastors to train an initial leadership corps and/or to overcome past small-group difficulties the church may have encountered.

*INTENSIVE SEMINAR*—A brief, quick seminar/workshop lasting one day, a weekend, but no more than three days; often conducted as a retreat; works well for all leadership levels; good method for quick start-ups and getting people going.

*ONE-ON-ONE*—Personalized training; individually meet with potential leaders, one or more sessions; works well for all leadership levels, especially small churches that don't have many leaders to train.

*APPRENTICE LEADER*—"Apprentice" with an experienced leader; "master teacher" concept, an experienced leader trains a new leader; works well for training small-group leaders, but it can also work with leadership leaders; a super method in large, ongoing group ministries.

*SELF-STUDY TUTORIAL*—Self-paced, mediated (books, manuals, video or audio tapes) presentation completed at the new leader's own speed; works well for all leadership levels; a good idea for small and large churches; be sure to monitor the leaders' progress and completion.

*"PROFESSIONAL" TRAINING*—Conference, workshop, or tailor-made training prepared and led by a paid small-groups consultant/expert; suitable for all leadership levels; a budget item; works better in churches with large-group ministries.

Choosing which training model to use depends on several things: the number of leaders you need to train; the leadership level (groups-ministry team, leadership leaders, or small-group leaders); the time and money available; and both the trainees' and the trainers' backgrounds. It isn't an easy decision. Feel free to experiment. Try several different training models before deciding on one or two to use on a more permanent basis. But even then, stay flexible.

---

### EDUCATION VERSUS TRAINING

Is there a difference between "education" and "training"? In my opinion, yes! Education is an expanding activity; starting with where a person is at, it provides concepts and information for developing broader perspectives and the foundations for making future analysis and decisions. On the other hand, training is a narrowing activity; given whatever a person's present abilities are, it attempts to provide specific skills and the necessary understanding to apply those skills. The focus is on accomplishing a specific task or job.

While I use the term *training* routinely in this handbook, it implies both concepts. Small-groups-ministry leadership requires both training and education. For the most part, preservice training focuses on training—the leadership job—while education plays the important role for in-service training. But please don't waste time worrying about whether you're conducting training or education. This distinction is only useful if it makes sense to you.

---

No one model works every time. So, include in the process you use to evaluate the various models these considerations: If the model *didn't* work well, was it because it didn't match with criteria outlined in the previous paragraph, or was it merely a case of poor planning and implementation? If the model *did* work well, why did it work and what characteristics do you need to repeat next time it's used?

Selecting an appropriate training model is only the preliminary task. Now, you need to determine the training content and settle many details associated with conducting the training. Let's first consider the content routinely included in preservice training and then look at what is often provided at in-service opportunities. Later, we will explore the more routine details.

Options for the content of preservice training include:

- Reviewing the biblical basis for small groups
- Defining *small group*
- Identifying how small groups fit into the Church's life and ministry
- Explaining the leader's role and responsibilities
- Planning and leading a small-group meeting
- Dealing with difficult group members (or other leaders)
- Accomplishing needed administrative details (reports, etc.)

Options for the content of in-service training include:

- Small-group developmental stages
- Group dynamics
- Models for sharing leadership among group members
- Worship alternatives suitable for small groups
- Group activity ideas (service, recreation, etc.)
- Evaluation strategies
- Counseling referral sources (if needed to help a group member)
- Many other topics suitable to the specific church situation

*Who does it?* After determining what to do, it becomes necessary to identify who is responsible for accomplishing the outlined training tasks. The basic options discussed at the start of this step—"Who's Responsible to Recruit and Train"—are still in effect (see page 121); go back and review that material with the training task in mind.

Asking who's responsible is an important question when planning training. To begin with, you need to decide if the same individual or individuals who plan the training are also going to conduct the training. Having the same people do both tasks isn't necessary. In some cases, the planners first select trainers and then ask them to participate in planning the training. In many small churches the people doing the planning also conduct the training, assuming the responsibility for the entire training event.

When it comes to preservice and in-service training, here again, the same or different individuals can plan and conduct these events. Large churches ought to use as many people as possible. Small churches cheer when one person is willing to accept the total task.

## Training Issues

To assist the trainers in doing their jobs, it's helpful to consider various issues associated with training. Consequently, the following topics represent key training concerns and necessary actions.

*What are suitable training dates and times?* This is a crucial question. You can plan and deliver outstanding preservice and in-service training opportunities and have no one show up. Avoid this problem by paying attention to the following recommendations:

1. Ask representative participants for dates and times when they can attend.
2. Stay away from dates close to public holidays and school vacations.
3. Avoid dates and times that conflict with other major church activities.
4. Select dates and times appropriate to the in-service or preservice agenda.
5. Knowing that everyone can't attend whatever dates and times are selected, pick options that assure the highest attendance and consider offering the training on more than one date and time.
6. If weekday evenings are selected, be sure starting and ending times permit adequate time for the participants to travel to and from their work or homes.
7. People often prefer one long day (but never longer than six to eight hours) over multiple shorter days (for example, two hours every Thursday evening for six weeks).
8. If the training involves rented facilities—retreat center, cabins, etc.—make certain you select available dates and times.
9. If using a paid small-groups consultant/trainer, select dates and times when he or she is available.
10. When evaluating the training, ask participants whether the selected dates and times were suitable for their personal needs.
11. Learn from your mistakes; if the dates and times didn't work, don't repeat the format again.
12. If and when necessary, and if everyone agrees, change previously announced dates and times if it means having greater participation.

*Where is the training held?* Most often churches use their own facilities. This keeps costs to a minimum and makes it easier on everyone. Yet, other locations are possible and perhaps preferred. Selecting the right training location depends very much on the training model utilized, whether it's preservice or in-service training; how many participants you expect; the training goals and objectives; the location's educational "quality" and suitability; and the participants' preferences (avoid "I don't like going there" locations). Keeping these things in mind, which of the following locations—other than your own facilities—might work as training locations for your groups-ministry leaders?

✓ Private homes
✓ Retreat/conference centers
✓ Private cabins in the mountains, at the beach, in the woods, etc.
✓ Hotel conference rooms
✓ Church camps
✓ Restaurants
✓ Bank or business conference rooms

You've found an appropriate setting to conduct your training if you can answer "yes" to a majority of the following dozen questions:

1. Does it "fit" the selected training model?
2. Is it conducive to the training goals and objectives?
3. Is it available on the desired dates and times?
4. Is the cost, if any, within your limits?
5. Is it large enough for all the anticipated participants?
6. Does it have an effective teaching/learning atmosphere?
7. Is the furniture appropriate, comfortable, and adequate?
8. Can people easily find it?
9. If needed, is food service available?
10. Are rest rooms and break facilities easily available?
11. Have you used it before and it worked?
12. Other questions related to your specific needs.

*How is the training managed?* Assorted issues are related to this *how* question. The first *how* is, how much money do you need or have to work with? This, naturally, is a budget question. If you were thinking ahead, back in step 1 you included training in your budget. If not, now is the time to finalize this important issue. Money, or actually the lack of money, often dictates what you can and cannot do when it comes to training models, resources, and facilities.

Another *how* requiring careful attention is the teaching/learning plan. How are you going to design the teaching/learning process? If you're using an outside small-group consultant/trainer, it's very likely he or she handles this issue. Nevertheless, you're wise to check with the trainer and "approve" what he or she plans to cover and the methods he or she intends to use. In most situations, however, you or someone on the planning team must determine the content, develop the teaching objectives, select teaching methods, and then organize these elements into an orderly plan. Time and space don't permit exploring all the possibilities available to accomplish this task, but a quick trip to your local Christian bookstore will put you in contact with numerous good books and other resources to help you develop effective teaching/learning plans.

One final *how* to consider: How are you going to structure the schedule or agenda? An agenda seeks to organize the teaching/learning process by sequencing the available time appropriate to accomplishing the planned teaching methods. A "good" agenda accounts for all the allotted time but permits some flexibility. Also included in good agendas are things like breaks, time for questions and answers, plus some time to allow the participants to evaluate the training. A last comment about time: Avoid unrealistic, rigid time expectations. The biggest mistake is trying to do too much in too little time.

*Is everything ready?* This question suggests several things associated with making certain necessary details are accomplished before actually delivering the planned training. So, just prior to beginning the training event, be sure the following details are in order:

- ✓ Any needed materials are ready and available (handouts, charts, overhead transparencies, name tags, paper, pencils, chalk or markers, etc.).
- ✓ Necessary equipment is set up and ready for use (overhead projector, VCR, movie projector, etc.).
- ✓ Required arrangements are in order (lighting, tables and chairs, registration materials, room temperature, etc.).
- ✓ The training staff, and any necessary support staff, are present and ready to begin (have them arrive at least twenty minutes early, if not sooner).
- ✓ In rented or borrowed facilities, know the specifics (rest-room locations, who to go to for help if needed, pay-phone location, sound system, cleanup requirements, etc.).

*What is done at the training event?* The time has come to conduct the training. Starting on time communicates the event's importance and models a time stewardship the leaders will hopefully pick up on and emulate. As you get started, conduct the training, and wind up, here are some things to remember:

- ■ As you get started, use an "icebreaker" to introduce yourself to the participants and the participants to each other.
- ■ Explain any "ground rules" you want in effect (freedom to go to the bathroom at any time, no reasonable questions are inappropriate, no smoking in the bathrooms, coffee is always available, etc.).
- ■ Follow the teaching/learning plan, but be flexible enough to meet the learners' needs, adjust for time, or compensate for unexpected events (VCR doesn't work, the bulb in the overhead blew out, etc.).
- ■ Affirm participants' involvement and comments with verbal and nonverbal feedback (good eye contact, saying "thank you," nodding your head in an approving manner, listening, etc.).
- ■ Watch your time (begin on time, don't forget breaks, keep the pace moving, and be sure to end on time).
- ■ Recognize accomplishment (certificates of completion, thank you letters, etc.).
- ■ Clean up after yourself (straighten furniture, clean the chalkboard, return equipment, leave the place in better condition than you found it).

# STEP NINE WORKSHEET: ENLISTING AND TRAINING LEADERS

Church Name: _MAIN STREET CHURCH_          Date: _____

9-1. *The person filling out this worksheet:*

Name: _ELAINE SWAN_

9-2. *Is an individual or group responsible for recruiting small-groups-ministry leaders?*

☒ An individual; please specify: _DEB HOWE (BUT ALL THE PLANNING TEAM MEMBERS WILL HELP)_

☐ A group; please specify (1) the persons' names, (2) their relationship to the planning team, and (3) how they are organized—which tasks they have.

| Name | Telephone Number |
|------|------------------|
| 1. | |
| 2. | |
| 3. | *(LIST THE PLANNING TEAM)* |
| 4. | |
| 5. | |
| 6. | |

What is their relationship to the planning team?

ONE AND THE SAME

How are the groups organized?

DEB HOWE WILL ASSUME THE RESPONSIBILITY

9-3. *What is the recruiting plan?* (Describe in as much detail as possible.)
1. PLANNING TEAM DISCUSSION AND PLANNING (WHAT, WHO, WHEN)
2. IDENTIFY POTENTIAL CANDIDATES (RECOMMENDATIONS FROM PASTORS, ELDERS, AND PLANNING TEAM)
3. INITIAL CONTACT AND SCHEDULE INTERVIEW
4. CONDUCT INTERVIEWS AND FOLLOW-UP
5. HAVE ELDERS APPROVE THE LEADERSHIP ROSTER

9-4. *When does the recruiting start and when is it ideally concluded?*

Start by (specify date): MAY 15

Conclude by (specify date): JULY 31

9-5. *How are potential leaders identified?* (List methods.)
RECOMMENDATIONS FROM PASTORS, ELDERS, AND PLANNING
TEAM MEMBERS

9-6. *Must leadership candidates receive either preapproval before contacting them or postapproval after they agree to serve?*

☐ No, neither type of approval is needed.
☒ Yes; please specify what approval is needed and how/when it's obtained:
ELDERS MUST APPROVE ALL CHURCH LEADERS, INCLUDING ALL
SMALL-GROUP MINISTRY LEADERS

9-7. *What requirements are the recruiters asked to follow when conducting the recruiting interviews?* (Please describe.)
—EXPLAIN WHY THEY ARE BEING APPROACHED
—USING THE APPROPRIATE JOB DESCRIPTION, EXPLAIN THE
  MINISTRY TASK
—ANSWER ALL QUESTIONS . . . NO ARM TWISTING
—GIVE THEM AT LEAST 10 DAYS (?) TO THINK AND PRAY
  BEFORE ASKING FOR THEIR DECISION

9-8. *Is an individual or group responsible for training small-groups-ministry leaders?*

☐ An individual; please specify:

☒ A group; please specify (1) the persons' names, (2) their relationship to the planning team, and (3) how they are organized—how the tasks are divided.

| Name | Telephone Number |
| --- | --- |
| 1. DEB HOWE (CHAIR) | 555-1414 |
| 2. DON SWAN | 555-1002 |
| 3. JEFF EDGAR | 555-2116 |
| 4. | |
| 5. | |
| 6. | |

What is their relationship to the planning team?

TEAM MEMBERS

How are the groups organized?
—HOWE WILL DO DETAILS (SCHEDULING, SET UP, ETC.) AND WORK WITH SWAN ON THE AGENDA
—SWAN WILL COORDINATE THE ACTUAL TRAINING
—EDGAR WILL ASSIST AS NECESSARY AND DO PRESENTATION ON RESOURCES

9-9. *What is the preservice training plan?* (Describe in as much detail as possible: training models, who is the teacher/trainer, the content covered, etc.)
—LEADERSHIP BASIC TRAINING=8 HRS FRIDAY EVENING, SATURDAY
—(SEE HOW ORGANIZED ABOVE)
—CONTENT AREAS: 1. THE VISION FOR SMALL GROUPS AT MAIN STREET CHURCH
2. YOUR ROLE AS A SMALL-GROUP LEADER
3. PLANNING AND LEADING A SMALL GROUP
4.
5.

9-10. *When are the scheduled dates, times, and locations for preservice training?*

Dates:
SEPT 2 AND 3

Times:
FRI 7-9:30 PM
SAT 9-NOON AND 12:45-3:30 PM (TWO 15-MINUTE BREAKS AND PROVIDE LUNCH)
Locations:

CHURCH, ROOM 300 (LOUNGE)

9-11. *What details associated with preservice training must be accomplished prior to offering the training events?* (Be as specific as possible—what? when? and by whom?)
X SWAN MUST FINALIZE THE TRAINING CURRICULUM EARLY ENOUGH TO PREPARE HANDOUTS AND OVERHEADS
X SCHEDULE ROOM—HOWE WILL DO THIS IMMEDIATELY
X BE SURE EVERYONE KNOWS WHEN AND WHERE . . . PUBLICITY, AND A PERSONAL REMINDER SENT TO THE PARTICIPANTS—ADAMS' JOB
X E. SWAN WILL DO THE ROOM SETUP AND ARRANGE FOR THE BREAK GOODIES AND LUNCH

9-12. *What is the in-service training plan?* (Describe in as much detail as possible: training models, who is the teacher/trainer, the content covered, etc.)

    X FOR THE FIRST YEAR, IN-SERVICE TRAINING IS COMBINED WITH FOUR LEADERS' MEETINGS MODELED AFTER McBRIDE'S "STP" IDEA (PAGE 161)

    X DEB HOWE IS RESPONSIBLE (WORKING WITH DON SWAN)

    X FOUR TOPICS THIS YEAR: (1) DEALING WITH DIFFICULT GROUP MEMBERS, (2) GROUP PLANNING TECHNIQUES, (3) PRAYER OPTIONS, AND (4) GROUP EVALUATION

9-13. *When are the scheduled dates, times, and locations for in-service training?*

Dates: NOV 6, FEB 5, APRIL 2, JULY 2

Times: SUNDAYS 5:30-6:55 (BEFORE THE EVENING SERVICE)

Locations: CHURCH, ROOM 300

9-14. *What details associated with in-service training must be accomplished prior to offering the training events?* (Be as specific as possible—what? when? and by whom?)

    —DON SWAN MUST WORK WITH DEB HOWE TO PLAN THE AGENDA . . . BY SEPT 1

    —PUBLISH AND DISTRIBUTE A MEETING/TRAINING CALENDAR GRACE ADAMS IS RESPONSIBLE TO COMPLETE THIS TASK BY SEPT 18

    —ASK DR. CARLSON AT GRACE UNIVERSITY TO CONDUCT THE FOUR TRAINING SESSIONS (40 MIN EACH) — DON SWAN WILL DO THIS BY THE END OF JULY

# STEP NINE WORKSHEET: ENLISTING AND TRAINING LEADERS

Church Name: _____ Date: _____

9-1. *The person filling out this worksheet:*

Name: _____

9-2. *Is an individual or group responsible for recruiting small-groups-ministry leaders?*

☐ An individual; please specify:

☐ A group; please specify (1) the persons' names, (2) their relationship to the planning team, and (3) how they are organized—which tasks they have.

| Name | Telephone Number |
|------|------------------|
| 1. | |
| 2. | |
| 3. | |
| 4. | |
| 5. | |
| 6. | |

What is their relationship to the planning team?

How are the groups organized?

9-3. *What is the recruiting plan?* (Describe in as much detail as possible.)

9-4. *When does the recruiting start and when is it ideally concluded?*

Start by (specify date):

Conclude by (specify date):

9-5. *How are potential leaders identified?* (List methods.)

9-6. *Must leadership candidates receive either preapproval before contacting them or postapproval after they agree to serve?*

☐ No, neither type of approval is needed.
☐ Yes; please specify what approval is needed and how/when it's obtained:

9-7. *What requirements are the recruiters asked to follow when conducting the recruiting interviews?* (Please describe.)

9-8. *Is an individual or group responsible for training small-groups-ministry leaders?*

☐ An individual; please specify:

☐ A group; please specify (1) the persons' names, (2) their relationship to the planning team, and (3) how they are organized—how the tasks are divided.

| Name | Telephone Number |
|------|------------------|
| 1. | |
| 2. | |
| 3. | |
| 4. | |
| 5. | |
| 6. | |

What is their relationship to the planning team?


How are the groups organized?


9-9. *What is the preservice training plan?* (Describe in as much detail as possible: training models, who is the teacher/trainer, the content covered, etc.)


9-10. *When are the scheduled dates, times, and locations for preservice training?*

Dates:

Times:

Locations:


9-11. *What details associated with preservice training must be accomplished prior to offering the training events?* (Be as specific as possible—what? when? and by whom?)

9-12. *What is the in-service training plan?* (Describe in as much detail as possible: training models, who is the teacher/trainer, the content covered, etc.)

9-13. *When are the scheduled dates, times, and locations for in-service training?*

Dates:

Times:

Locations:

9-14. *What details associated with in-service training must be accomplished prior to offering the training events?* (Be as specific as possible—what? when? and by whom?)

## STEP TEN
# PROMOTING SMALL GROUPS

**OVERVIEW**—This step is designed to assist you in:

1. Recognizing the need for a realistic, workable promotion strategy.

2. Clarifying the small-groups-ministry vision—the message.

3. Deciding on specific promotional methods.

*And we proclaim Him, admonishing every man*
*and teaching every man with all wisdom,*
*that we may present every man complete in Christ.*
COLOSSIANS 1:28

**H**ow do the adults in your church find out about the small-groups ministry? You invest blood, sweat, and tears in planning the small-groups ministry, but if no one joins a small group, you've wasted your time and effort. Get the point? Promotion is both a reality and a necessity. Consequently, it's necessary to invest adequate time and effort in developing a realistic, workable promotion strategy.

Hiam and Schewe define *promotion* as "any technique that persuasively communicates favorable information about a seller's product to potential buyers; includes advertising, personal selling, sales promotions, and public relations."[1] While it needs some "tweaking" to fit small-group ministries, this terrific definition provides useful categories to include in your promotional strategy: (1) advertising, (2) personal "selling," (3) "sales" promotions, and (4) public relations. But before starting to devise a promotional plan, a few prior items need your attention.

*Why promote small groups?* Promotion's aim is to ensure that everyone who needs to know about the small-groups ministry does in fact know. But knowledge isn't the only purpose. Promotion also seeks to have people "buy" the product. In your context that means having people join the groups you're planning. In short, promotion attempts to communicate the value and benefits associated with the groups ministry as it impacts the total church—or an identified segment—and the individual participants.

*Who's in charge of promotion?* Devising and implementing the promotional plan must be someone's specific responsibility, but whose? Is one person or a committee in charge? Recalling our earlier discussion on recruiting and training, there are several alternatives available for the planning team to consider. Refer to the seven options outlined on page 122. The advice offered earlier is still appropriate and applicable to the promotion task.

*What's the message?* What do you want to communicate to people about your small-groups ministry? The methods you use to promote the ministry are only as good as the content or message you seek to communicate. An ideal message seeks to get attention, hold interest, arouse desire, and obtain action—in short, to foster group membership and participation. In practice, few messages are able to take your adult members all the way from awareness to action. You may need to use different messages in your promotional mix at various stages along the promotional trail.

A message has both content and format. To start, you need to clarify what you want to say and then identify methods to communicate the message. Your message must honestly state, in a positive manner, the small-group vision. More on this topic later.

*What "givens" are you working with?* Your promotional strategy is directly affected by the numerous decisions you made in previous steps; namely, how the groups ministry fits into your church's overall ministry, the specific goals that provide direction for the ministry, the level of application, what type of groups you want to develop, and the many details associated with implementing the groups. Each prior decision provides background upon which to base the promotional content and procedural decisions. There's no way I can identify everything this implies. Nevertheless, you're wise to keep this information in the back of your mind.

*Is there a difference between persuasion and manipulation?* Some people become nervous when I talk about promotion. They fear manipulating people. This is a legitimate fear. However, I make a distinction between persuading people and manipulating people. It's a simple distinction, but very useful. In general, my responsibility in ministry is to persuade or influence people to accept and follow Jesus Christ. To persuade is to convince. Specifically, my motivation is to change their knowledge, attitudes, opinion, and behavior—in short, to prompt them to join a group—so they benefit, actually so we all benefit, as members of God's family. On the other hand, manipulation seeks to influence people's behavior in order to derive benefit for myself without regard for their well-being. Applying these thoughts, I definitely want to persuade—not manipulate—people to participate in a group.

## FORMULATING A PROMOTION STRATEGY

Formulating an effective promotional strategy requires several phases. As you progress through each suggested phase, don't forget to *write down* the decisions you make. A written plan is useful in communicating your intent to others, directing the plan's implementation, and providing a record for future reference. So, don't leave anything to memory. Write it down.

Informing the adults in your church about the groups ministry is not particularly controversial. However, when you attempt to persuade them to join a group, you risk irritating and even alienating some individuals. Go slow, don't push. Persuasion isn't arm twisting. Pursue only their best interests. Use persuasive promotion to advance the groups ministry, not to cause ill will or conflict. But this is a difficult challenge, requiring the planning team's full attention.

The phases are presented in a logical order. However, your unique situation may require a different order and different elements. Ready, let's begin.

### Phase One

*Clarify the vision*, that is, your promotional message. It's tough to "sell" a product—the groups vision—if it's something you're not excited about. Enthusiasm is contagious. Therefore, clearly defining the small-groups vision is a requirement preceding any promotion efforts. After all, you can't effectively promote a "product" you don't know and understand (or at least don't try to know and understand).

According to George Barna in his book *The Power of Vision* (Regal Books, 1992), "Vision is a picture held in our mind's eye of the way things could or should be in the days ahead. Vision connotes a visual reality, a portrait of conditions that do not exist currently." Vision is "foresight with insight based on hindsight." What do you want the small-groups ministry to become in your church?

Your groups vision began back in the first steps when you conducted a context audit and completed the needs assessment. These activities led to establishing the groups-ministry goals—what you want to accomplish, why you think groups are necessary. Wrap this all up in a short statement and you have your vision.

Promotion focuses on presenting vision. Consequently, please follow these principles:

- "Sell" the vision, not the small-groups program. Stress the biblical rationale, the reasons behind small groups, plus the individual and church benefits.
- Ensure that the vision is realistically (and honestly) presented.
- Clearly articulate the vision in a manner whereby church and community members understand and catch the vision for themselves.
- Persist and persevere in communicating the vision.
- Most importantly, promote the vision focusing on glorifying God.

Phase one is complete after you translate the vision into *promotion objectives*: brief statements that identify what you want to accomplish in promoting the small-groups ministry. In general, the promotional strategy seeks to inform, persuade, and remind. But there's more to it. Promotion objectives usually focus on action over an extended period—first making members/regular attenders aware of the groups ministry and then building interest, desire, and ultimately their decision to participate. Once they're participating, the objectives can also include promoting "goodwill" (see phase 7).

**Phase Two**
*Determine what resources are available and needed.* Once again, you must turn your attention to a subject that frequently appears as you develop the small-groups ministry—resource allocation. By now you know the term *resources* means more than money; it also includes time and "talent" (people). Throughout the planning process you're required to balance these three items. Promotion is no exception.

Promotion alternatives are controlled to an extent by how much money you have to work with. Consequently phase two has two potential paths to follow: (1) plan whatever promotional methods you think are suitable, find out how much money they cost to execute, and then ask for the needed resources; or (2) find out what financial resources you have and then plan a promotional strategy within these boundaries. The second option is the most realistic for nearly all small-groups-ministry planning teams.

Money isn't the only cost associated with developing your promotional strategy. Talent or personnel is a second consideration. Some promotional methods require significant experience and expertise. Knowing what talent exists in your church or community—willing and available talent you can utilize—can either expand or constrict your promotional alternatives. In some cases, available talent is accessible without cost. Utilizing some people, however, means paying *very* high fees. But this is rare. Most talented Christians are willing to lend a hand if they are asked correctly and have the time available. For example, a highly talented commercial artist donates her time and abilities to create a series of posters that communicate the small-group vision.

Time is the third budget item. Timing is everything when it comes to your promotional strategy. Having a promotional schedule and sticking to it is mandatory. This is such an important consideration it gets its own phase, phase four.

### Phase Three

*Planning promotional elements and methods.* "Promotional elements" refers to advertising (and publicity), personal "selling" (one-on-one methods), and sales promotion (events)—the first three subheadings included in the promotion definition stated earlier. The fourth element, public relations, constitutes phase 7.

Each element lends itself to a variety of appropriate methods. Some methods are inexpensive and easy to use, while others are quite costly and demand considerable expertise. In most situations, a mixture of elements and methods usually produces the best results.

Just a reminder before continuing on: To select the best method within each promotional element, keep in mind: (1) the small-groups vision, (2) what you know about your congregation and community, (3) available resources (money, time, and talent), and (4) the small-groups-ministry application level.

### *Advertising*

Advertising is any impersonal, structured communication about ideas, goods, or services paid for by an identified sponsor. This definition sounds rather scary and, perhaps to some, inappropriate for promoting small-group ministries. But with a little tailoring and explanation it suits our purposes just fine.

The "ideas, goods, or services" in our case, of course, is the small-groups-ministry vision, plus the related benefits associated with group membership and participation. "Paid for by an identified sponsor" simply refers to identifying the church as the sponsoring organization. It's the phrase "impersonal, structured communication" that causes most people to pause. "Structured communication" suggests advertising is an orderly attempt to convey persuasive information, to cause the "consumers" to "buy the product" (the adult church members to join small groups). The word *impersonal* merely connotes methods that are not tailored to each specific member in the church or application level. Rather, the methods are general in nature, aimed at everyone in general and no one in specific.

Advertising normally utilizes the mass media—newspapers, magazines, television, radio, direct mail, etc. As you plan the advertising element in promoting the small-groups ministry, here are some "mass media" options you might consider using:

- Weekly church worship folder
- Church newsletter
- Denominational newsletter
- Brochures
- Posters
- Local Christian radio station
- Public-access cable television

- Mailings to church members/regular attenders
- Mailings to Christian community groups
- Community newspaper

While you needn't be an advertising expert, here are a few ideas or concepts, not necessarily the specific terms, you may find useful as you think about advertising your small groups ministry:

ADVERTISING MARKET refers to the specific audience at which the advertising message is directed—your groups-ministry application level. Depending on whom you're targeting—the whole church or a specific segment—knowing about your "market" helps you tailor and communicate an effective message.

ADVERTISING PLATFORM alludes to the small-group issues and benefits you wish to convey in the advertising message. Like a political platform, it includes all the "planks" (reasons) to "vote" (join) for the candidate (small groups).

ADVERTISING CAMPAIGN denotes the message with a single theme that is repetitively communicated to the "target audience" over a prolonged time. An advertising campaign must fit in and complement the overall promotion strategy.

ADVERTISING THEME means the slogan or central idea that is repeated throughout the advertising campaign. For example, "a caring community"; "Care and be cared for in a Caring Group"; "Think small, join a Growth Group"; etc.

PUBLICITY is a form of advertising that focuses on communicating the organization's message through the mass media, but it costs the organization nothing (it's free). Most church advertising is really publicity. However, on occasion, you may elect to spend the necessary amount to buy time on local radio or television stations.

A final note about advertising. In the secular world advertising has its dark side. I'm sure you can come up with many illustrations of how advertising is dishonest, manipulative, and exploitative. However, even though there is a possibility of abusing its ideas and methods, advertising can be a useful tool in promoting your small-groups ministry. Just proceed with caution.

### Personal "Selling" (One-on-One Promotion)

Without a doubt, the best way to promote your small-groups ministry is sharing the vision with people one on one. In advertising terms, this is "personal selling." At its best, personal, one-on-one methods are really "direct marketing." That is, (1) a specific, definite offer is made—join a small group; (2) all information necessary to make a decision is provided; and (3) a method for responding is given—fill out the registration card, etc.

One-on-one strategies are ideal because the message can be tailored to the specific individual or, in some situations, to the small group. It has the greatest potential for helping people see the values associated with small-group membership. Here are a few good applications:

- In the person's home, or if appropriate, at his or her office or work
- Presentation to an adult-education class (ladies' group, Bible study, etc.)
- Having a cup of coffee with a friend
- A telephone call
- Conversation while participating in a task or recreation
- Your suggestions:

### *"Sales" Promotion*

When was the last time you went to the grocery store? I'll bet as soon as you walked through the front door you were bombarded with posters and displays proclaiming numerous products. This is an example of "sales promotion." Samples, coupons, contests, premiums, rebates, trade shows, etc., are all considered sales-promotion methods. Sales promotions are usually intended to increase sales over a short period, while personal selling and advertising have a long-term sales goal. Translated into small-groups-ministry terms, this means short-term ideas or events aimed at quickly promoting the small-groups ministry.

"Sales" promotions are the least-used promotion method in the church. Nevertheless, they have their place in a well-thought-out promotional mix. Can you think of anything else besides the options listed below?

- A small-groups booth in the church lobby
- A one-night, "visit-a-group" opportunity
- A video shown after the morning worship service
- A small-groups booth at a "ministries fair"
- A contest to see which group can be first in "birthing" a new group

### Phase Four

1. Having a promotion strategy is great, but who exactly is responsible to put what into action and when?
2. When is the best time (hour, day, month, season, etc.) to implement the various elements in your promotion strategy?
3. How long (days, weeks, months, years) does the promotion last?
4. What time lines and deadlines must be established and kept in order to implement the promotion strategy?
5. Does the plan/schedule conflict, compete, or interfere with other church events or promotional activities?

### Phase Five

*Secure the necessary approval.* In some churches this phase is essential; others may simply disregard this detail. Approval or permission to proceed and implement the promotional strategy is frequently an issue within highly structured, highly organized churches. Often at stake are financial considerations: "Yes, we want to do it, but we don't have the money right now." If your context requires securing some kind of approval to proceed, do it; failure to secure it can lead to calamity!

Is there someone who must approve your promotional plan? If yes, who, how, and when? Don't proceed until these questions are answered satisfactorily!

### Phase Six

*Implementing the strategy.* This is the "doing-it" phase. Putting the promotional strategy into action involves two considerations: preparing the methods and putting the strategy to work.

*PREPARING THE METHODS.* Knowing which methods you want to use, and when you intend to use them, is obviously important, but a vital issue still remains: preparing or getting the method ready for utilization. As you write the copy, lay out the format, tape the segment, or whatever, follow these preparation principles:

✓ Be complete and thorough.
✓ Do it right! Quality, quality, quality!
✓ Meet all required deadlines. Time is valuable!
✓ Run all concepts and ideas by several people to get their reactions.
✓ Retain the right to edit everything.
✓ Proof everything twice.
✓ Hold people accountable to do their assigned tasks and to do them well.
✓ Don't exceed your resource limits.
✓ Reduce costs and save money if possible.
✓ In case something goes wrong, be prepared with alternative "plan B."

*Putting the strategy to work.* Ready, get set, go! With plan and schedule in hand, it's time to implement the promotional strategy. Some words to the wise:

✓ Stay flexible, but stick to the plan and schedule.
✓ If the plan and schedule aren't working, make any needed alterations before too much time and money are wasted.
✓ Once started, finish the job in style. Do your best!

## Phase Seven

*Follow-up public relations.* In my way of thinking public relations (PR) is an ongoing promotional activity. Therefore, I include it as the final promotion phase you need to consider. By definition public relations is "a promotional activity that aims to communicate a favorable image of a product or its marketer and to promote goodwill."[2] "Goodwill" represents the potential for the small-groups ministry to earn favor and status as an important element in the church's life and ministry. It is the sum total of both objective and subjective criteria. Goodwill results from "customer" acceptance, ministry effectiveness, reputation, quality, efficiency, leadership competency, and financial stability. As you can imagine, these factors cannot always be programmed, but come through continuing effort.

Follow-up PR seeks to maintain a positive image for the groups ministry. Positive, ongoing PR is what you want and need. The goal is to keep the ministry before the people in a constructive fashion. Therefore, here are possible methods to try:

■ Testimonials
■ Reporting positive events in the church newsletter
■ Quickly dealing with any difficulty that may arise
■ A commissioning service for small-groups-ministry leadership
■ A written and visual "annual report"
■ Your suggestions

Sometimes PR, and so-called goodwill, can be negative. Adverse publicity has damaged group ministries that allowed dysfunctional groups to persist, incompetent leaders to remain in leadership, deviant doctrine to cause church splits, personality clashes to rend groups, etc. Unfavorable PR can lead to people's dropping out, or worse yet, disbanding the groups ministry altogether. When and if possible, think ahead and ward off anything that may cause problems. Unfortunately, circumstances that you have no control over will result in unfavorable PR. When it happens, learn from the experience and avoid repeating it.

To summarize, PR is an ongoing process that seeks to:

- ✓ Maintain or enhance the small-groups ministry
- ✓ Build loyalty and support for small groups
- ✓ Attract prospective new leaders
- ✓ Provide information about successes
- ✓ Attract potential new group members
- ✓ Correct inaccurate or incomplete information about the groups ministry

---

NOTES
1. Alexander Hiam and Charles D. Schewe, *The Portable MBA in Marketing* (New York: John Wiley & Sons, 1992), page 440.
2. Hiam and Schewe, page 440.

# STEP TEN WORKSHEET: PROMOTING SMALL GROUPS

Church Name: __MAIN STREET CHURCH__          Date: _____

10-1. *The person filling out this worksheet:*

Name: __GRACE ADAMS__

10-2. *Is an individual or group responsible for promoting the small-groups ministry?*

☐ An individual; please specify:
☒ A group; please specify (1) the persons' names, (2) their relationship to the
planning team, and (3) how they are organized—how the tasks are divided.

| Name | Telephone Number |
|---|---|
| 1. GRACE ADAMS (CHAIR) | 555-4142 |
| 2. LUCIE PEREZ | 555-6831 |
| 3. LYDIA WONG | 555-5222 |
| 4. | |
| 5. | |
| 6. | |

What is their relationship to the planning team?
A SUB-COMMITTEE (GRACE IS A TEAM MEMBER)

How are the groups organized?
—GRACE IS CHAIRING THE GROUP AND COORDINATING WITH THE
PLANNING TEAM
—LUCIE IS RESPONSIBLE FOR POSTERS
—LYDIA IS CREATING OUR BROCHURE ON HER COMPUTER

10-3. *What is the vision for small groups?* (Phase 1)
AS PER THE PLANNING TEAM: "SMALL GROUPS: YOUR OPPORTUNITY
TO HELP ONE ANOTHER GROW IN CHRIST, EXPERIENCE MUTUAL
CARING, AND BECOME PART OF THE MAIN STREET FAMILY."
PROMOTION OBJECTIVES: —REACH EVERY MEMBER AND REGULAR
ATTENDER WITH THE SMALL-GROUP MINISTRY OPPORTUNITY
—UTILIZE EVERY PROMO METHOD AVAILABLE IN OUR CHURCH

10-4. *What resources are available and needed?* (Phase 2)
$210 WAS BUDGETED FOR PUBLICITY . . . WE ARE GOING TO USE THE
MAJORITY OF THIS ON ART SUPPLIES FOR POSTERS AND PRODUCE A
SIMPLE BROCHURE TO PHOTOCOPY.

10-5. *What* advertising *elements are included in the promotion strategy?* (Identify and describe.)

—WEEKLY WORSHIP BULLETIN—GRACE WILL COORDINATE WITH THE CHURCH SECRETARY

—MONTHLY CHURCH NEWSLETTER ("CHURCH NOTES")—GRACE WILL ALSO HANDLE THIS

—BROCHURE . . . LYDIA'S JOB

—POSTERS . . . LUCIE'S JOB


10-6. *What* one-on-one *elements are included in the promotion strategy?* (Identify and describe.)

—DON SWAN WILL TALK WITH ALL ADULT CLASS LEADERS AND ENLIST THEIR SUPPORT

—THE PLANNING TEAM IS GOING TO DIVIDE UP THE MEMBERSHIP LIST AND ATTEMPT TO GIVE EVERYONE A PHONE CALL

—THE TEAM IS COMMITTED TO "CASUALLY" TALKING WITH EVERYONE IN OUR CHURCH THEY INTERACT WITH


10-7. *What* "sales" promotion *elements are included in the promotional strategy?* (Identify and describe.)

—SMALL-GROUPS BOOTH IN THE CHURCH LOBBY

—DON IS GOING TO ASK MR. BROWNLEE IF HE'LL PRODUCE A FIVE-MINUTE VIDEO TAPE "COMMERCIAL"

—GRACE IS GOING TO ASK PASTOR ODEN IF THE TEAM CAN HAVE 5 MINUTES TO DO A "SKIT" IN THE MORNING WORSHIP SERVICES, LAST SUNDAY IN JUNE, JULY, AND AUGUST


10-8. *What is your promotional schedule?* (Phase 4) (Be as specific as possible.)

—PROMOTION BEGINS IMMEDIATELY AFTER THE ELDERS APPROVE THE SMALL-GROUPS MINISTRY PLAN . . . BY JUNE 1ST

—POSTERS UP AND BROCHURES OUT BY JUNE 15TH

—CHURCH NEWSLETTER . . . MEET PUBLICATION DEADLINE, CHECK WITH THE CHURCH SECRETARY (JUNE, JULY, AUGUST, SEPT)

—WEEKLY BULLETIN STARTING IN JUNE

—EVERY MEMBER (AND REGULAR ATTENDERS IF POSSIBLE) PERSONALLY CONTACTED BY THE END OF AUGUST

—ALL CLASS LEADERS CONTACTED BY THE MIDDLE OF JULY

10-9. *What approval, if any, is necessary prior to implementing the promotion strategy?* (Phase 5) (Who? What? When?)

    ELDERS GAVE THEIR APPROVAL ALREADY TO DO AS WE SEE NECESSARY

10-10. *What special methods or tasks must be prepared or accomplished prior to implementing the promotion strategy?* (Phase 6) (Identify and describe: What? Who? When?)

    —MAINLY FINISHING THE BROCHURE . . . LYDIA IS GOING TO SUBMIT HER MOCKUP TO THE PLANNING TEAM BY THE END OF MAY

10-11. *What is the plan for continuing follow-up public relations?* (Phase 7) (Describe in as much detail as possible: What? Who? When?)

    —WE WANT TO HAVE A REGULAR COLUMN IN THE CHURCH NEWSLETTER ABOUT "MAIN STREET GROUPS"—PASTOR ODEN AND DON SWAN
    —LAST SUNDAY IN EACH MONTH THE PASTOR HAS SAID WE CAN PRESENT A "GROUP TESTIMONY" . . . GRACE WILL COORDINATE THIS

# STEP TEN WORKSHEET: PROMOTING SMALL GROUPS

Church Name: _____ Date: _____

10-1. *The person filling out this worksheet:*

Name:_____

10-2. *Is an individual or group responsible for promoting the small-groups ministry?*

☐ An individual; please specify:
☐ A group; please specify (1) the persons' names, (2) their relationship to the planning team, and (3) how they are organized—how the tasks are divided.

| Name | Telephone Number |
|------|------------------|
| 1. | |
| 2. | |
| 3. | |
| 4. | |
| 5. | |
| 6. | |

What is their relationship to the planning team?

How are the groups organized?

10-3. *What is the vision for small groups?* (Phase 1)

10-4. *What resources are available and needed?* (Phase 2)

10-5. *What* advertising *elements are included in the promotion strategy?* (Identify and describe.)

10-6. *What* one-on-one *elements are included in the promotion strategy?* (Identify and describe.)

10-7. *What* "sales" promotion *elements are included in the promotional strategy?* (Identify and describe.)

10-8. *What is your promotional schedule?* (Phase 4) (Be as specific as possible.)

10-9. *What approval, if any, is necessary prior to implementing the promotion strategy?* (Phase 5) (Who? What? When?)

10-10. *What special methods or tasks must be prepared or accomplished prior to implementing the promotion strategy?* (Phase 6) (Identify and describe: What? Who? When?)

10-11. *What is the plan for continuing follow-up public relations?* (Phase 7) (Describe in as much detail as possible: What? Who? When?)

STEP ELEVEN
# MANAGING SMALL GROUPS

**OVERVIEW**—This step is designed to assist you in:

1. Explaining the ongoing management function in small-groups ministries.

2. Discovering various management methods and techniques.

3. Selecting appropriate management systems.

*Let all things be done properly and in an orderly manner.*
1 CORINTHIANS 14:40

**M**anagement, by my definition, is the process of working with and through others to achieve ministry goals in an efficient and effective manner. This simple definition introduces the main thrust in step 11—working with and through others to achieve your small-groups-ministry goals. More specifically, achieving those goals in an efficient (methods) and effective (results) manner.

Once the small-groups ministry is under way, the task shifts from planning to managing. As an ongoing activity, managing the small-groups ministry is best accomplished by design rather than by default. By this I mean doing things in a deliberate manner, not in a reactionary, last-minute, or "winging-it" fashion. A successful small-groups–ministry plan must include intentional systems—organized procedures—to assist the ministry in gaining and maintaining vitality.

Volumes are written on management. This step isn't designed to make you a management expert. Rather, it's designed to help you think about and plan workable systems to implement two broad concepts—administration and development—as applied to your small-groups ministry.

## ADMINISTRATION

Administration is the process of directing systems and their related procedures to accomplish ministry goals. Does this sound a bit abstract? It needn't. "To furnish help or be of service," is one dictionary's definition for *administer*. I like it! Administration, then, is people-centered activity designed to help or serve those people active in the groups ministry—both leadership and group members. Administration is aimed at achieving those small, not-so-glamorous, routine details necessary to make the groups ministry succeed.

Details if left unattended can possibly multiply and short-circuit the system. For example, the church is using the same study book in all its relationship-oriented small groups, but no one ordered the books and they're needed starting tonight. Oops! Someone overlooked a small but important detail. Whose job was that, anyway?

Administration is very much dependent upon and must reflect your distinctive situation, your exact small-groups ministry. Not every situation needs or wants the same administrative system and requirements. The general principle is: "Keep it simple, saint" (KISS; some people use "stupid" for the last *s*, but this isn't appropriate in group ministries). There is no need to create an administrative monster that takes a life unto itself, demands excessive personnel, and gobbles up large quantities of time. Beware!

Forewarned about potential pitfalls, you should know that administration seeks to (1) identify procedures needed to sustain the groups ministry, (2) organize the identified procedures into logical systems, and (3) assure timely compliance/completion. Administration is a tool to help the groups ministry, not a rope to bind or restrict the ministry. Flexibility, reality, and simplicity must characterize all administrative systems.

Administration is an expansive topic that goes beyond this handbook's limits. So to help us gain a beginning perspective, and to apply it to group ministries, I divide the topic down into three subdivisions: *coordination, supervision,* and *strategic planning.*

## Coordination

Coordination is a communication process to maintain unity and harmony in the small-groups ministry's day-to-day operations. Put another way, coordination is the sum total of all activities directed at making sure everyone knows what's going on and how he or she is affected. The purpose is to build "oneness," unity in the minds and actions of everyone involved in the groups ministry. Coordination is communication!

Coordination mainly deals with things, ideas, and information. Do leaders and group members know what they need to know concerning the groups ministry? When is the next leadership in-service training event? Do leaders have the resources they need? How long can Hank lead the group before he's transferred to Denver? When does the next new group start? Why are the groups limited to from fifteen to twenty members? Answers to these and many other questions represent the necessity for coordination.

Coordination requires both horizontal and vertical communication lines. *Horizontal coordination* seeks to integrate and synchronize purpose, activities, resources, dates, times, etc., among the individual group leaders and between the group leaders and the members in their groups. *Vertical coordination* is communication between the individual group leaders and those providing overall leadership for the groups ministry. It entails communicating purpose and vision, ministry requirements, administrative details, etc., plus any necessary horizontal coordination among the groups and/or group members.

*How is coordination done?* Very carefully! It's no joke, coordination can either greatly enhance a small-groups ministry's success or severely impede its progress. Consequently, here are some possible coordination techniques you may find achievable in your context:

- One-on-one meetings
- Leaders meetings
- Ministry procedures manual
- Church and/or group calendars

- Leadership mailboxes
- Letters and memos
- Leadership notice board in the church office
- Telephone calls
- Small-groups newsletter
- Your suggestions:

## Supervision

Supervision is the process of supervising people—to provide oversight, direction, and evaluation. Where coordination deals with ideas and information, supervision focuses on helping the small-groups-ministry leaders succeed. Coordination is needed if supervision is to succeed. However, supervision more narrowly focuses on helping leaders do their specific jobs. The goal is to (1) equip leaders, (2) motivate and encourage leaders, (3) ensure compliance with group-ministry administrative expectations, and (4) assist in evaluating the leaders' performance as leaders. It may sound a little harsh, but supervision is there to help leaders do what they are supposed to do.

Ask people at work who is accountable for their supervision, and they usually can tell you. It's the person to whom they report, to whom they go for assistance; the person who helps them do their job to the best of their abilities. Likewise, small-group–ministry leaders at all levels need a supervisor—someone to come alongside and provide needed assistance, encouragement, and to hold them accountable for accomplishing their ministry at the highest level possible. Ultimately, supervision is serving servants.

Caution is needed at this point. While some similarities do exist, supervising small-group leaders isn't exactly like supervising someone in the workplace. Volunteer ministries are just that, volunteer positions. There is no paycheck or continued employment to hold over anyone's head. In supervising, supervisors must demonstrate humility (Philippians 2:3), a servant's heart (Matthew 20:28), and care for those whom they serve (1 Corinthians 12:25).

Who supervises whom? This question was addressed in part back in step 8 when you determined the leadership levels required for your groups ministry. But at this point it may be helpful to clearly distinguish the likely supervisory relationships (certainly other options are possible):

| *Leadership Level* | *Likely "Supervisor"* |
|---|---|
| Small-groups-ministry team | Pastor, elders, deacons, etc. |
| Leadership leaders | Small-groups-ministry team |
| Small-group leaders | Leadership leaders |

Job descriptions are the supervisor's essential tools. These written statements outline who is responsible to do what. The supervisor uses the descriptions to guide his or her interaction with the supervisees. Everyone knows the expected job requirements, and this becomes the basis for a leader's self-evaluation and his or her assessment by the appropriate supervisor. This necessary performance evaluation is designed to help, not find fault and criticize. More is said about evaluation in our last step, step 12.

How does one go about supervising within a groups ministry? The specific answer to this question, of course, depends on your specific situation. Supervision methods that work in one church won't necessarily work in all churches. Here are some methods you may find workable in your context:

- One-on-one meetings (breakfast, coffee break, home visit, etc.)
- Self-evaluation reports (verbal or written; fill out a "form")
- Buddy system (leaders are paired together)
- Visiting group[1]
- Group meeting reports (verbal or written; fill out a "form")
- Formal evaluation reports (verbal or written; fill out a "form")
- Your suggestions:

*Should I require written reports?* Perhaps one of the most useful tools you have to coordinate information and indirectly supervise leaders is the written report—especially if you're dealing with a very large, diverse small-groups ministry. This method is useful only if it's easy to accomplish and relevant to the task. That is, avoid involved reporting systems that demand excessive information and are time-consuming to complete. Likewise, reports may not be necessary every week. Consider using written reports when fifteen or more individual groups are involved. Many different applications are possible. Below is one example.

---

### CARING GROUP WEEKLY REPORT

Group ID: _____ Designated Leader: _____

Date Group Met: _____ Time: _____

Number in Attendance:

Prayer Requests:




Needed Resources and/or Information:



Signature: _____ Date: _____

---

Written reports commonly take two forms: predesigned (like the weekly report, example above) or free-form (just provide the requested information on a blank sheet of paper). I recommend a predesigned form. The information you ask for on the form depends on what you want to know. Note the example: It asks for prayer requests and anything else the leaders needed. Furthermore, design a system that's simple to administer. For example, give the leaders a handful of the forms a couple times per year and place a return box in the church library.

Don't be surprised if your leaders fall behind in completing their reports. This is very common. However, don't let it become a habit. Likewise, if the written reporting system isn't working, think about adjusting it or doing away with it altogether.

I haven't mentioned reporting systems for other leadership levels. If you have a large small-groups ministry you might want to consider some kind of reporting system for your leadership leaders. Furthermore, does the small-groups–ministry team need to submit written reports to anyone? Even if the answer is no, I'd recommend a yearly, written report to the pastor and governing board.

*How often do I hold leaders' meetings?* One method I find useful is to hold regular meetings that include all leadership levels. "Regular" can mean different things to different people. Some small-group advocates suggest weekly meetings. This works well in highly structured group ministries if (1) the leaders were recruited knowing that they are required to attend, and (2) it's an important element in how the groups operate—that is, leaders meet with a master teacher and then return and teach the same content in their respective groups. But in my opinion, weekly gatherings are overkill—it's too much if you expect your leaders to function well in their specific ministries. The ideal frequency, in my experience, is quarterly (four times per year). At the most, and in most cases, avoid having leaders' meetings more than once every six to eight weeks.

The meeting format that works best for me is what I call STP (Sharing, Tips, and Prayer). Held each quarter, the format includes sharing successes and struggles the leaders are experiencing, plus any information relevant to all the leaders (coordination); tips on group issues (education and training); and prayer. The event lasts one and a half hours and everyone is required to attend. It's an upbeat meeting that is designed to inform, encourage, and motivate.

Separate meetings for each leadership level may be necessary. These meetings can be in addition to the regular STP meeting or a segment of the STP meeting. But regardless of the format and frequency you select, avoid having too many meetings. Then make sure that what meetings you do have are well planned and executed. Your leaders will come, the majority of the time, if they think the meetings are worth their time. See to it that they are!

## Strategic Planning

Strategic planning is an important, ongoing management function. Someone has said that it's leadership's first responsibility. By definition, strategic planning is the process of developing a plan designed to pursue what the groups ministry wants to become, given the church's internal strengths and external opportunities. The result of strategic planning is a logical strategy for accomplishing its defined goals and objectives.

Strategic-planning activities focus on the future: how a church should move from its current small-groups-ministry status to achieve the desired groups-ministry goals. Planning establishes the links between the church's overall strategies and its small-groups-ministry strategies. It is concerned with how to integrate all group-ministry decisions into a coherent overall small-groups strategy that complements the church's future plans. Additionally, both church and small-groups-ministry leaders face decisions on how to structure the groups ministry as it grows and develops, whether to centralize or decentralize the leadership functions, what type of groups to include or exclude, future leadership needs, and the role group ministries play in the church's future.

The planning associated with building a small-groups ministry—the topic explored in this handbook—is preliminary to strategic planning. It gets things started. Some call this initial planning "program planning." But whatever you want to call it, it serves as the basis for ongoing strategic planning aimed at maintaining and growing the groups ministry once it's under way.

All the planning procedures and methods at your disposal cannot be dealt with in this handbook. Consequently, you need to look elsewhere and find a planning model suitable to your context and needs. Go to your local bookstore and look under the church-administration section. You're likely to find several suitable books or manuals. Another alternative is to see what is available in the library at your local Bible college. Of course, you can always use a planning model you know about from work or school, as long as you tailor it to the specific needs in your church.

Strategic planning is an ongoing process, not a one-time shot. Likewise, it isn't an optional activity if you're serious about a continuing, vital small-groups ministry. As you begin and maintain a well-designed planning process, here are a few guidelines:

✓ Start planning today!
✓ Find a planning model/design you understand and can use.
✓ Be as thorough as possible.
✓ Include as many people as possible in the ongoing planning process.
✓ Be flexible!
✓ Remind yourself: a strategic plan is a guide, not a set of handcuffs.

Okay, let's assume you have a planning model in hand and ready to use. Now what? There is more than one way to facilitate the planning process. Various methods are at your disposal. Listed below are some examples:

■ Individual group calendars
■ Yearly church planning retreat
■ Leadership planning retreat
■ Church calendar/groups calendar
■ Planning sheets passed out to all leaders
■ An agenda item at routine and/or special-groups-ministry team meetings
■ Your suggestions

## DEVELOPMENT

Development, specifically leadership development, is any attempt to improve current or future leadership performance by imparting knowledge, changing attitudes, or increasing skills. It provides the small-groups ministry with ongoing leadership growth and improvement.

The ultimate aim for development is, of course, to glorify God by equipping Christians to minister effectively. Secondarily, but in specific, it's designed to enhance the small-groups ministry's present and future effectiveness—to meet the stated goals. As a result, the development *process* seeks to (1) assess and meet the groups ministry's leadership needs (for instance, to fill future leadership leader openings) by (2) appraising the current leaders' performance and needs and then (3) providing opportunities for the leaders to develop their entry-level and ongoing leadership knowledge and skills.

Development is an important ongoing administrative function for several reasons. The main reason is that small-groups-ministry leaders are volunteers from among the adult members/regular attenders in your church. As such, many do not already possess the desired knowledge and skills required to serve effectively. A never-ending development plan seeks to address this situation. Similarly, leadership development facilitates organizational continuity by preparing leaders and current group members to smoothly assume "higher" level positions within the groups ministry. Development also helps "sensitize" leaders to the importance of small groups in the church and their needed leadership role.

A typical small-groups-ministry development program involves several steps. First, a ministry projection is made; here you project your leadership needs based on factors like planned expansion or turnover in present leaders. Next the planning team (or in the long run the small-groups-ministry team) reviews the various leadership levels—small-groups-ministry team, leadership leaders, and small-group leaders—and develops leadership knowledge and skills requirements: what leaders need to know and be able to do to succeed in their respective ministries. Next, this information is used to plan appropriate education and training opportunities. Seminars, courses, workshops, self-paced workbooks, etc., are then developed to provide the needed educational/training content. Lastly, an evaluation procedure is implemented to assess the leaders' knowledge and skill, and to determine future development needs. The basic process just described is a never-ending cycle.

### Education and Training

Education and training are perhaps the two most easily identified development activities. Back on page 128, I suggested a distinction between education and training. Education is an expanding process to equip people with the knowledge and understanding necessary to analyze and make decisions, whereas training is a narrowing activity to equip people to do a specific task. Both are needed; both are important to sustain a quality small-groups ministry. Some individuals, however, prefer calling only education "development" and putting training in its own category. Whatever. In this handbook we lump them together.

Both preservice and in-service training are essential elements. Again referring to page 128, preservice training focuses on equipping leaders with the basic information and skills necessary to get started in their respective ministries. In-service training, on the other hand, attempts to expand the leaders' knowledge and broaden their insight into small-group ministries.

Small-groups-ministry management must include leadership training on a continuing basis. Therefore, ongoing administrative systems designed to facilitate planning, implementing, and evaluating training must be established and maintained. To do this, continue the training process the planning team began back in step 9. All the information related to training presented in step 9 is utilized to maintain a quality development program (system).

*How often should training be offered?* An important question; the frequency issue deserves careful attention. Too much training and the busy volunteers who lead the small-groups ministry become frustrated and, in the face of everything else, often choose not to participate. Too little training and people feel isolated, unprepared, and are likely to abandon ship at the earliest opportunity. So, what's the answer? As you heard before, "It all depends." It depends on the number of leaders you presently have (or will start with), your groups-ministry growth rate (how many new leaders are needed?), and your groups-ministry turnover rate (how many new *replacement* leaders are needed?). Like nearly everything else associated with an effective groups ministry, the answer depends on your situation. Nevertheless, to help you make this important decision, here are three options for preservice training:

1. Assuming the need is present, offer an intensive "basic training" (six to eight hours) two or three times per year.
2. Offer "basic training" once each year.
3. Have ongoing preservice training via one-on-one strategies.

And here are three options for in-service training:

1. Offer one or two training opportunities each quarter at various times.
2. Offer it twice per year (September and February?).
3. Offer at least one training "event" (retreat, etc.) per year.

Remember, a classroom isn't the only suitable site for training. There are many other ways or settings in which to provide quality training. Besides the methods suggested in step 9, here are some alternatives you may wish to utilize:

- Supervised "on-the-job training" (OJT)
- Coaching by a leadership leader
- Leadership skill workshops
- Computer-based training
- Articles and books
- Special training events (Serendipity, regional Sunday school conventions, etc.)
- Seminars with small-group consultants/trainers
- Your suggestions

Before considering our second development issue, recognition, I'd like to share with you several tips related to designing and managing a training system for small-groups ministry:

- Informal atmosphere and methods seem to work best. Avoid formal "school" methods as your *only* approach to training.
- Within the training, vary your content and presentation methods to meet your learners' needs. Tailor "canned" presentations to the situation.
- Pay attention to the learning atmosphere (location, lighting, seating, temperature, handicapped access, etc.).
- Require attendance at preservice and in-service training—write the requirement into the job description and be sure the expectation is covered during the recruiting interview.
- Schedule training regularly, but only as needed. A good idea is to establish a regular training schedule (every quarter, twice per year, etc.) at consistent dates, times, and places. Doing so helps people plan ahead.
- Consider using a familiar system to structure and promote your training (for example, Equipping University, commonly referred to as "Equipping U.").
- Promote your training events. Make certain everyone knows.
- Be a good steward; don't waste people's time; be well prepared.
- Begin and end on time; and don't forget breaks!
- Light refreshments, or lunch if an all-day event, are appropriate.
- Provide recognition—a "Certificate of Completion."
- Follow up on nonattenders to find out why they missed (but be nice).

## Recognition

An important aspect of managing a small-groups ministry is recognizing people's accomplishments. Appropriate, adequate recognition is an important player in developing present and future leaders. It isn't fluff, it's a necessity.

Recognition is acknowledging, approving, and/or appreciating faithful service—giving credit where credit is due. Not flattery (to praise excessively without conviction or sincerity) or an award (a contest, examination, or skills prize), recognition is something given or done in return for merit, service, or achievement. The purpose is to honor and affirm the leaders' ministries. Few if any leaders who donate their time and effort expect anything in return. Nonetheless, I like to think of recognition as a "payment" for well-rendered service. As volunteers, they deserve being "compensated."

Over the years I've made these observations about giving suitable recognition:

- Recognition is biblical. Passages like Romans 12:10; 1 Corinthians 3:8, 12:23; and 2 John 8 all connect service with reward or honor.
- Recognition demands the giver's genuine attitude and action. Avoid just going through the motions to grant recognition that lacks sincere, heartfelt appreciation.
- Recognition demands timely conferral. This one is obvious—be sure to give the deserved recognition at a time closely related to the accomplishment.
- Recognition must be presented in a suitable context (at an appreciation banquet, commissioning service, etc.).
- Recognition needs tailoring to the individual. Some people are highly motivated by, and want, public recognition. Others eschew any public spotlight. The type and method of recognition must be suitable for the individual to whom it is given.
- Recognition doesn't demand expensive gifts; it's truly the thought that counts.
- Recognition is a requirement for successful small-group ministries!

Ask yourself: "What type of recognition would I like given to me?" If you would appreciate one of the following expressions of recognition, perhaps others might also find it gratifying:

- Simply saying thank you
- Handwritten thank you notes
- Gift certificates from a local Christian bookstore
- Appreciation desserts or dinners
- Certificates of appreciation (suitable for framing) or engraved wall plaques
- Their "story" or personal profile in the church newsletter or worship folder
- Commissioning services
- Christian books or videos
- Continuing telephone contacts to see how they are doing

---

NOTE
1. Use very sparingly! If you do, be sure to join in and participate in group activities. Avoid overt language or actions that appear judgmental. No surprise visits; make certain the leader knows in advance you're coming.

# STEP ELEVEN WORKSHEET: MANAGING SMALL GROUPS

Church Name: MAIN STREET CHURCH      Date: _____

11-1. *The person filling out this worksheet:*

Name: DON SWAN _____

11-2. *Is the small-groups-ministry team (or equivalent) responsible for managing the groups ministry?*

☒ Yes
☐ No. Specify who is responsible and describe how the various responsibilities are divided up:

11-3. *What coordination methods are needed?* (Describe what and how.)
—EACH GROUP MEMBER WILL HAVE DIRECT CONTACT WITH A SMALL-GROUPS MINISTRY TEAM MEMBER (THEIR "COACH")
—COACHES WILL CONTACT THE GROUP LEADERS AT LEAST ONCE EVERY TWO WEEKS
—ALL GROUP LEADERS (AND TEAM MEMBERS) HAVE MAILBOXES IN THE CHURCH OFFICE
—STP FOUR TIMES THIS YEAR (SEE WORKSHEET 9, PAGE 135.)

11-4. *What supervision is necessary in the small-groups ministry?* (Describe what and how.)
—THE SMALL-GROUPS MINISTRY TEAM WILL ALSO SERVE AS "LEADERSHIP LEADERS" AND SUPERVISE THE INDIVIDUAL SMALL-GROUPS LEADERS
—GOING TO ASK FOR SIX-MONTH AND FINAL WRITTEN REPORTS (SWAN WILL DEVELOP THE FORM)

11-5. *When it comes to supervising the small-groups-ministry leadership, who supervises whom?* (Identify the supervisory relationships.)
THE PLANNING TEAM HAS AGREED TO BECOME THE ONGOING SMALL-GROUPS MINISTRY TEAM (BUT FRANK WASHINGTON IS REPLACING JEFF EDGAR WHO IS MOVING) . . . DON, FRANK, AND ELAINE WILL "COACH" TWO GROUP LEADERS

11-6. *Will written reports be used as a coordination/supervision tool?*

☐ No
☒ Yes (describe or attach a copy):
—AT SIX MONTHS (PROGRESS REPORT)
—AT THE END (EVALUATION REPORT)
      EACH ONE PAGE IN LENGTH (DESIGNED BY DON)

11-7. *What leadership meetings are included in managing the small-groups ministry?*
*(Please describe.)*
4 "STP" MEETINGS (SHARING, TIPS, AND PRAYER) THE
PURPOSE IS TO COORDINATE INFORMATION AND CHURCH
EVENTS RELATED TO THE GROUPS MINISTRY, PROVIDE IN-SERV-
ICE TRAINING, MOTIVATE AND ENCOURAGE, AND PRAY FOR
ONE ANOTHER AND THE GROUPS MINISTRY IN GENERAL . . .
SWAN IS RESPONSIBLE

11-8. *What strategic planning process is included in managing the small-groups*
*ministry?* (Please describe.)
THE PLANNING TEAM WILL SPEND 15-20 MINUTES ON STRATE-
GIC PLANNING AT EACH OF THEIR REGULAR MEETINGS . . .
FRANK (OUR NEW TEAM MEMBER) IS AN EXPERT ON THIS
TOPIC AND WILL PROVIDE LEADERSHIP IN THIS PROCESS

11-9. *In addition to the preservice and in-service training planned in step 9, what*
*additional education and training is included in the ongoing management plan?*
*(Please describe.)*
—ENCOURAGE ATTENDANCE AT THE MID-LAND SS CONFER-
ENCE
—CREATE A SMALL-GROUPS RESOURCE CENTER IN THE
CHURCH LIBRARY
—ASK ELDERS FOR SCHOLARSHIPS TO ATTEND THE SERENDIPITY
ADVANCED CONFERENCE

11-10. *How will recognition be utilized in managing the small-groups ministry?*
(Identify and describe: What? Who? When?)

—PROFILE A GROUP AND ITS LEADERS IN EVERY OTHER EDITION OF THE CHURCH NEWSLETTER

—DON WILL SEND HANDWRITTEN "THANK YOU" NOTES TO ALL GROUP MINISTRY LEADERS, GROUP LEADERS, AND CHURCH STAFF AT THE END OF THE YEAR

—HAVE A GROUP LEADERSHIP DESSERT

11-11. *Are there other small-groups-management issues, unique to your context, that must be addressed?*

☐ No
☒ Yes (specify and describe):
THE ELDERS WANT TO KNOW HOW MANY ADULTS ARE ATTENDING THE GROUPS . . . THEY ARE ASKING FOR A MONTHLY REPORT. EACH COACH WILL GATHER THIS INFO FROM THEIR GROUP LEADERS AND GIVE THE DATA TO DON WHO WILL INFORM THE ELDERS

# STEP ELEVEN WORKSHEET: MANAGING SMALL GROUPS

Church Name: _____ Date: _____

11-1. *The person filling out this worksheet:*

Name: _____

11-2. *Is the small-groups-ministry team (or equivalent) responsible for managing the groups ministry?*

☐ Yes
☐ No. Specify who is responsible and describe how the various responsibilities are divided up:

11-3. *What coordination methods are needed?* (Describe what and how.)

11-4. *What supervision is necessary in the small-groups ministry?* (Describe what and how.)

11-5. *When it comes to supervising the small-groups-ministry leadership, who supervises whom?* (Identify the supervisory relationships.)

11-6. *Will written reports be used as a coordination/supervision tool?*

☐ No
☐ Yes (describe or attach a copy):

11-7. *What leadership meetings are included in managing the small-groups ministry?* (Please describe.)

11-8. *What strategic planning process is included in managing the small-groups ministry?* (Please describe.)

11-9. *In addition to the preservice and in-service training planned in step 9, what additional education and training is included in the ongoing management plan?* (Please describe.)

11-10. *How will recognition be utilized in managing the small-groups ministry?*
(Identify and describe: What? Who? When?)

11-11. *Are there other small-groups-management issues, unique to your context, that must be addressed?*

☐ No
☐ Yes (specify and describe):

# EVALUATING SMALL GROUPS

*Let each one examine his own work,*
*and then he will have reason for boasting*
*in regard to himself alone, and not in*
*regard to another.*
GALATIANS 6:4

**OVERVIEW**—This step is designed to assist you in:

1. Discerning the role evaluation plays in a small-groups ministry.

2. Identifying the evaluation sequence—information, judgments, decisions—as it fits into your situation.

3. Deciding on an evaluation method and what, when, and where to conduct the evaluation.

Evaluation is among the most neglected and unused tools available to help build small-group ministries. It's commonly misunderstood and deemed unspiritual. Nevertheless, it is a valuable process. This last planning step, step 12, is designed to assist you in devising a basic evaluation plan. A much more in-depth look at evaluation is presented in chapter 7 of my book, *How to Lead Small Groups* (NavPress, 1990). At this point my intent is to introduce the topic and set you on the right course.

Evaluation as a concept and process carries different meanings for different people. For our purposes, I define evaluation as *the systematic process of obtaining information and using it to form judgments, which in turn are used in decisionmaking.* Let's look a bit more closely at the ideas contained in this definition.

*INFORMATION* is the data or facts you need to begin the evaluation process; it's the raw material. Timely, accurate information is essential. This necessary information is obtained from various sources related to the evaluation's focus. "Junk in, junk out" is definitely true when dealing with evaluative information.

*JUDGMENTS* are informed estimates or opinions based on the available facts. They are initial determinations that provide the basis for making final decisions. Specifically, judgments estimate the present situation or predict future performance. More than one judgment is possible for any given set of information.

*DECISIONS* are the final product in evaluation. They're rulings or conclusions on what actions are needed in response to the related judgments. Each judgment may produce one or more decisions. The goal is to make rational, reasonable choices based on informed judgments—which are dependent, of course, on whether reliable information is received.

Here are two examples of information, judgments, and decisions that constitute the evaluation process:

### Example A

*INFORMATION:* Four leadership leaders report on their written evaluations that they don't have enough time to adequately coach (supervise) ten small-group leaders.

*JUDGMENT:* If four out of six leadership leaders report difficulty coaching ten small-group leaders, the "span of control" is too large. Reduce the number of group leaders each leadership leader coaches.

*DECISION:* Reduce the number of group leaders coached by each leadership leader down to seven; recruit and train three new leadership leaders.

### Example B

*INFORMATION:* Sixty-two percent of the group members disagreed with the requirement that all groups had to remain "open" and accept new members during the entire year they met together as a group.

*JUDGMENT:* A majority of group members feels strongly about not requiring all groups to remain open.

*DECISION:* Allow each group to decide for themselves whether or not they will remain "open" or "closed" after the sixth meeting and remain a fixed group for the remaining time they're together as a group.

Evaluation is implemented at two different levels or times: (1) *formative evaluation*, during the time the groups are meeting, to assure the groups ministry is on track toward meeting its goals; and/or (2) *summative evaluation*, at the end of the training. While the groups are meeting, evaluation provides feedback useful in making midstream corrections (see example A above). Evaluation near the end of the groups' life cycle tells you how it went and provides data useful in making future improvements (example B).

*Who is responsible for evaluation?* Ah yes, once again you face the "who does it" question. And once again the answer depends on your context and leadership structure. While many people may get involved, in most churches the small-groups-ministry team, or equivalent group, maintains the overall responsibility for planning, implementing, and using the evaluation results. If this isn't true in your church, please clarify who is responsible and make sure they're doing their job.

*Why evaluate?* Before moving on, you need to stop to consider why evaluation is a needed element in the small-groups ministry. Being personally persuaded that evaluation is important assists you in helping others see its value. So, why evaluate? Here are four reasons; add any others you like:

1. *It's a biblical mandate.* While evaluation isn't directly commanded in Scripture, the idea or concept is clearly advocated. Words such as *judge, test,* and *examine* are used to convey the idea (see Psalm 26:2; 2 Corinthians 13:5; 1 Thessalonians 2:4, 5:21).

2. *Evaluation promotes quality.* Quality, effective small-group ministries don't happen by chance. Evaluation is a tool to assist you in meeting your groups-ministry goals. Are you doing or did you do what you set out to accomplish? Honest evaluation helps you to check out your own efforts, other leaders' efforts, and the ministry in general; it identifies areas of strength and alerts you to any needed changes.

3. *Evaluation builds accountability.* Everyone must be held accountable for his or her

responsibilities and tasks. Even if you're only answerable to yourself, evaluation provides a means whereby you can assess your own efforts.

4. *Evaluation provides the basis for making responsible decisions.* Pragmatically, this is a very important justification for evaluation. Flimsy information and snap judgments usually produce poor decisions. However, decisions that come from a careful evaluation, rather than anecdotal data or personal bias, provide a reliable basis for choosing between alternatives. If asked to explain your decisions, you'll have logical reasons to offer.

*What is evaluated?* Evaluation focuses on various aspects of the small-groups ministry—it requires information. Is information needed on the overall small-groups ministry or for a specific leadership level or programmatic sub-element? No matter what the specific focus, the evaluation process must seek information by asking and answering the basic questions: How is it going (formative evaluation), or how did it go (summative evaluation)? To do this, relevant questions are asked in at least three essential categories:

### Goals
How did it go (or is it going)—in terms of meeting your *goals?* Examples:

- *Did twenty prospective new group leaders attend and complete "basic training"?* Information needed: Attendance figures and completion rates.
- *Are the participants who finished the training able to explain how the small-groups ministry fits into our church's life and ministry?* Information needed: Feedback on whether or not the trainees can adequately explain how the small-groups ministry fits into our church.

### Participant Attitudes and Opinions
How did it go (or is it going) in terms of *participants' attitudes and opinions* toward their leadership role and/or experience in a small group (group format and agenda, interaction, acceptance and "belonging," leadership, time, location, etc.)? Examples:

- *In most participants' opinions, which topics discussed did they think were the most helpful?* Information needed: Participants' opinions on which topic was the most helpful.
- *Do the small-group leaders think in-service training is worth their time?* Information needed: Participants' opinions on whether or not they think the in-service training was worth their time.

### Details
How is it going (or did it go) in terms of the planning, administrative, and implementation *details*—for the individual groups and/or the entire small-groups ministry? Examples:

- *Are the leadership meetings held at a convenient time?* Information needed: Feedback on scheduling conflicts; alternate times available; participants' opinions.
- *Were adequate efforts made to publicize "basic training"?* Information needed: Participants' opinions and feedback from the person responsible for publicity.

Questions are your guides in evaluation. They provide direction in several ways. First, they permit you to identify what information you want and need. Second, based on the information you want, questions facilitate developing an appropriate evaluation questionnaire or interview. Third, they provide the basis upon which your judgments and decisions are made. And lastly, questions provide a logical format for presenting your decisions to those individuals who need the results.

Questions are written in the present, past, or future tenses to reflect formative or summative evaluation. Just make certain you understand their intent and use. For example, here is one of the previous example questions written in all three tenses:

- Past tense: *Did the small-group leaders think in-service training was worth their time?*
- Present tense: *Do the small-group leaders think in-service training is worth their time?*
- Future tense: *Will future small-group leaders think in-service training is worth their time?*

In writing questions, feel free to use the method and form that works for you. No one method is right or wrong. However, be sure to make the questions pertinent, to the point, as short as possible, and understandable to those answering. The aim is to formulate questions that help secure the information needed to evaluate your overall small-groups ministry and any chosen sub-elements.

*What evaluation methods are used?* Considering your specific situation, one or more of the following evaluation strategies is possible:

INFORMAL VERBAL FEEDBACK—Casually ask individual leaders (at all levels) and participants for their opinions on relevant issues. This may occur during routine conversations, at breaks during training, at group meetings, after attending a leaders' meeting, or whenever it's appropriate. But, be cautious. Feedback of this sort is often anecdotal and doesn't necessarily represent everyone's opinion on the issue.

FORMAL VERBAL FEEDBACK—Whether talking in groups or with individuals, structure a systematic interview to ask leaders and/or participants the same specific questions and receive their verbal replies. Interviews may be conducted with individuals or groups. One interesting option is to hold a "public meeting." This "town hall" approach works fairly well, but usually only a small percentage of the leaders (unless they're required to attend) and group members participate. Most people, but not all, prefer offering anonymous evaluation feedback.

WRITTEN FEEDBACK—Based on what you want to know—the information you're seeking—design a questionnaire that's completed by the leaders and/or group members. This method is commonly used at regular intervals during the groups' life cycle, when the groups are coming to an end, at training events, at leadership meetings, after a specific training session, at the end of each day when a multiday training or planning format is used, etc. Questionnaires are the most commonly used, also the most abused, evaluation method. If you elect to use written feedback methods, please consult other resources besides this handbook.

INSTANT FEEDBACK—If the trust level is high between leaders and other leaders, leaders and group members, and group members and other group members, an excellent option is to invite spontaneous evaluation comments during the event, meeting, training, etc. If this is to work, begin building trust by inviting this form of feedback during the time you're presenting the ground rules, and then continually reinforce the idea by occasionally asking questions like, "How did that go?" or "What did you think about this session or activity?"

It's often impractical to receive verbal or written feedback from every individual or group, especially when there are numerous people, leaders, and groups. A workable alternative is to use the desired evaluation methodology with a small "representative" sample of groups or individuals. Distribute the questionnaire or make an appointment with each randomly selected group or individual. Using samples to represent the total opinion is a common event in our society. Nevertheless, it's a process that requires a certain knowledge and expertise. If you don't personally meet this requirement, find someone in your church to lend a hand or find a book or manual to help you.

In many churches the ideal strategy is to use more than one evaluation method. For instance, one church I'm familiar with asks each small group to discuss defined evaluation questions and have a group member prepare a one-page summary. Added to this is a questionnaire completed by each small-group leader. Both the group questions and leader's questionnaire ask some similar questions and a few additional questions appropriate to the specific respondents. All the information is pooled and the top-level leadership team (what I've been calling the small-groups leadership team) uses the data in forming judgments and making decisions. In turn, the decisions are implemented in the next planning cycle. Their evaluation system doesn't work perfectly all the time, but it's way ahead of doing nothing and merely flying blind.

Regardless of the method you use, feedback from your participants provides up-to-date information. Its downside lies in the fact that people often are either too polite or, in some cases, too harsh in their evaluations. The questions you use or don't use make a big difference. Your word choice and sentence structure are important. Likewise, structured or "forced-choice" questions (multiple-choice, yes-no, rankings, etc.) are usually more useful than open-ended questions (for example, "What was your favorite activity?"). Structured questions are more easily tabulated and analyzed. But once again, please seek help if you're not experienced in writing questionnaires or structuring interviews.

Don't be shy. If you need some assistance in constructing your interview or questionnaire, head for your local library or bookstore. Is there someone in your church who has the knowledge and experience to help you?

## Collecting the Data
*When and where is the evaluation information collected?* You know what you want to ask and how you plan to ask, but now you must determine when and where to ask.

*WHEN:* The specific time or times must fit these criteria:

1. Select a date and time while the groups, training, and leaders meeting are still in progress (formative evaluation).
2. Select a time when the training event is finished, the meeting is over, or groups are concluding. This is the most common point at which evaluation is usually conducted (summative evaluation).
3. Select a date a few weeks after the group, meeting, or training is finished. It's advantageous at times to wait a short while, so the leaders and participants can

reflect on their experience, prior to asking for their evaluations.

4. Select a time when other agenda items don't distract from or cause postponing the evaluation altogether.
5. Select a time that allows enough time to finish the questionnaire or interview.

*WHERE:* Where is the evaluation information collected? The most obvious answer is at the location where the groups meet, the training is held, etc. In some cases it may be possible to mail a questionnaire and have respondents mail it back after they complete it (be sure to include a postage-paid return envelope). However, if you use an evaluation questionnaire at the end of a meeting or training event, think twice before you allow the participants to take it home to fill out. They're likely to forget to complete it, let alone send or bring it back.

If you're following the third criterion above, consider using either the U.S. mail to send out evaluation questionnaires, or when possible (usually smaller churches), call each leader and/or participant on the telephone. You're wise if you previously told them you were going to contact them in this fashion.

*What are the recommended judgments and decisions?* When the data has been collected and reliable evaluative information is in hand, then it's appropriate for those individuals responsible for the evaluation to (1) analyze the data and (2) formulate judgments and decisions.

*ANALYZE THE DATA*—Analyzing the data normally takes one of two different avenues: a descriptive analysis or a statistical analysis. A descriptive analysis is the most practical option and the easiest to accomplish. The aim is to clearly describe your results. Using words and some numbers—such as averages and percentages—describe the evaluation information. The following statement is a good example:

*Of the participants who completed the evaluation questionnaire, 88 percent thought the training was worth their time.*

The second option is a formal statistical analysis. Questions dealing with the significant differences between responses, correlations, and predictive equations are all possibilities. Obviously this second option requires help from someone who is knowledgeable in this area. Time and space don't permit us to explore this alternative. However, don't dismiss this option too quickly; it's useful in situations where you are dealing with business persons and other professionals.

*FORMULATE JUDGMENTS AND DECISIONS*—Actually, this step began prior to this point. It has occurred informally from the very beginning. However, now it's time to formalize the process based on the collected information.

Each previously identified evaluation question implies related judgments and decisions. Judgments are informed estimates or opinions based on the available facts, the information at hand. Then, based on those judgments, decisions are rulings or conclusions on what action is needed in response to the related judgments.

Making judgments and decisions is straightforward at times. For example, it doesn't take a rocket scientist to determine the best course of action when confronted with information that tells you group members like selecting their own meeting time—allow them to select their own meeting time. In other circumstances, however, the judgments and decisions aren't clear and demand total reliance on God's leading as you determine the best course of action.

On occasion, the actual judgments and decisions may not be your responsibility at all; you're only responsible for gathering the information, making initial judgments, and suggesting nonbinding decisions. Someone else—a pastor, committee, board, etc.—is the final decisionmaker.

*Who needs to know about the decisions (evaluation results)?* In a few instances no one other than the small-groups-ministry team needs to know about the evaluation results (decisions). However, in most situations many other people need access to the results. Ask yourself, "Who needs to know and why?" This question implies several things. First, those who conducted the evaluation need to identify the individuals who would like to receive or must receive the results. Second, the reasons for needing to know, which may vary, must be clarified. Some individuals need to know only for informational purposes. Others require the input because they in turn need to make related decisions and/or the final decisions.

In practice, it's a good idea to avoid appearing secretive when it comes to the evaluation results. One good practice, if appropriate, is to publish the results in your church newsletter. In doing so you inform the individuals who participated in the evaluation, undergird the rationale for any forthcoming decisions or actions, and elevate the evaluation's present and future role. It's always wise to let anyone have whatever evaluation information he or she wants. Perhaps the only exception to this rule is specific performance information collected while assessing the various leadership levels. This really isn't "public" information and deserves closer protection.

*How are decisions (evaluation results) communicated?* The method chosen to communicate the decisions is very important. Usually, it's a good idea to utilize both written and oral communication methods.

Written report—Clearly written evaluation reports needn't be long and complicated. Precise and concise presentations employing charts and graphs are preferred. Written reports are best because they provide a tangible evaluation record. In turn, this record documents your small-groups ministry and serves as a future reference source.

Oral presentation—An oral presentation or report provides the opportunity to describe, explain, and if necessary, sell the results. Oral presentations may include brief conversations or formal presentations to larger groups. However, it's rarely a good idea to trust in oral reports alone. People fail to hear, forget, or even change the facts. An oral report coupled with a written report is *always* your best choice.

## PUTTING IT ALL TOGETHER

You've come to the finish line. Step 12 concludes the planning cycle for building a small-groups ministry. If you followed my suggestion to read through this handbook before beginning the actual planning process, it's time to put together your own plan. If, however, you've been formulating your plan all along the way, it's time to see if it floats. Either way, may God bless your efforts.

As you can find the time, look over the various items included in the appendixes. You'll find many good ideas.

# STEP TWELVE WORKSHEET: EVALUATING SMALL GROUPS

Church Name: MAIN STREET CHURCH      Date: _____

12-1. *The person filling out this worksheet:*

Name: DON SWAN

12-2. *Is the small-groups-ministry team (or equivalent) responsible for developing the evaluation plan?*

☒ Yes SWAN IS
☐ No; then please specify who is responsible and describe how the various responsibilities are divided up:

12-3. *Why is evaluation included in a small-groups-ministry plan?* (Explain in your own words.)

THE MINISTRY TEAM FULLY REALIZES THE NECESSITY FOR EVALUATION IF GROUPS MINISTRY IS TO GROW AND SUCCEED. . . . A METHOD TO LEARN WHAT IS GOING WELL AND WHAT ISN'T

12-4. *What additional resources are available to help plan the small-groups-ministry evaluation?* (List evaluation topics you need additional help with; books, articles, manuals, etc., you have or need to find.)

| Topics | Resource |
| --- | --- |
| GENERAL EXPLANATION | CHAPTER 7 IN HOW TO LEAD SMALL GROUPS |

ELAINE SAID SHE WILL GO TO THE LIBRARY AT THE CHRISTIAN UNIVERSITY AND SEE IF THEY HAVE ANY HELPFUL MATERIAL ON EVALUATION METHODS AND PROCEDURES

12-5. *What must be evaluated?* (Identify goals, participants' attitudes and opinions, and details or anything else you wish to evaluate.)

—GROUP ADMINISTRATIVE DETAILS (PLACE, TIME, DAY)
—IS THE GROUP MEETING THE STATED GOALS?
—THE GROUP'S FORMAT AND AGENDA
—GROUP MEMBERS' PARTICIPATION
—SUGGESTIONS FOR IMPROVEMENTS (ANY AREA)

12-6. *What formative and summative evaluation is needed?* (Describe based on the answer given for question 12-5.)

BOTH ARE NEEDED . . .
    X FORMATIVE AT ABOUT 6 MONTHS
    X SUMMATIVE AT THE END OF THE FIRST YEAR

DON IS DEVELOPING A ONE-PAGE QUESTIONNAIRE THE LEADERS CAN USE AS THE BASIS FOR DISCUSSION IN THEIR GROUPS AND THEN COMPLETE AND TURN IN (THE SAME FORM BOTH TIMES, TO ALLOW FOR COMPARISON)

12-7. *Depending on how question 12-6 was answered, what evaluation method or methods will be used?* (Identify and describe.)

—ASKING THE GROUP LEADERS TO CONDUCT AN INFORMAL EVALUATION DISCUSSION(S) IN THEIR GROUPS AND THEN TO SUBMIT A WRITTEN REPORT(S) (LEADERS TRAINED TO DO THIS AT THE NOV "STP" MEETING)
—SUBMIT WRITTEN REPORT TO THEIR COACH, WHO IN TURN WILL REVIEW THEM AND PASS THEM ON TO DON SWAN

12-8. *When will the data (information) be collected?* (Identify dates and times.)

TWICE: AT 6-MONTHS AND AFTER ONE YEAR
#1 DISCUSSION AT A JANUARY MEETING . . . REPORT BY THE END OF JANUARY
#2 DISCUSSION AT A JULY MEETING . . . REPORT BY THE END OF JULY

12-9. *Where will the data (information) be collected?* (Please describe.)
   —GROUP DISCUSSIONS
   —LEADER REPORTS (TWICE)

12-10. *How will the data information be analyzed?* (Describe.)
   —SIMPLE TALLY AND DESCRIPTION
   —THE MINISTRY TEAM WILL DETERMINE IF ANY ACTION(S) IS/ARE NEEDED AFTER THE FIRST REPORT (EVALUATION DISCUSSION AND REPORTS) AND UNDERTAKE ANY NEEDED "SYSTEM" ADJUSTMENTS

12-11. *Who must receive the evaluation results?* (Identify persons to receive the results.)
   —MINISTRY TEAM
   —ELDERS
   —GROUP LEADERS
   —CHURCH (IN NEWSLETTER ARTICLE)

12-12. *By what methods are the evaluation results communicated?* (Identify and describe.)
   —WRITTEN SUMMARY REPORT . . . DON SWAN'S TASK
   —DON WILL ALSO GIVE ORAL REPORTS TO THE ELDERS, TEAM, AND GROUP LEADERS
   —TWO ARTICLES (WRITTEN BY GRACE ADAMS) IN CHURCH NEWSLETTER

# STEP TWELVE WORKSHEET: EVALUATING SMALL GROUPS

Church Name: _____ Date: _____

12-1. *The person filling out this worksheet:*

Name: _____

12-2. *Is the small-groups-ministry team (or equivalent) responsible for developing the evaluation plan?*

☐ Yes
☐ No; then please specify who is responsible and describe how the various responsibilities are divided up:

12-3. *Why is evaluation included in a small-groups-ministry plan?* (Explain in your own words.)

12-4. *What additional resources are available to help plan the small-groups-ministry evaluation?* (List evaluation topics you need additional help with; books, articles, manuals, etc., you have or need to find.)

*Topics* _____ *Resource* _____

12-5. *What must be evaluated?* (Identify goals, participants' attitudes and opinions, and details or anything else you wish to evaluate.)

12-6. *What formative and summative evaluation is needed?* (Describe based on the answer given for question 12-5.)

12-7. *Depending on how question 12-6 was answered, what evaluation method or methods will be used?* (Identify and describe.)

12-8. *When will the data (information) be collected?* (Identify dates and times.)

12-9. *Where will the data (information) be collected?* (Please describe.)

12-10. *How will the data information be analyzed?* (Describe.)

12-11. *Who must receive the evaluation results?* (Identify persons to receive the results.)

12-12. *By what methods are the evaluation results communicated?* (Identify and describe.)

# ADDITIONAL RESOURCES

## DEFINING "SMALL GROUP"

Writers in the field of group dynamics do not agree completely on a definition for small groups. However, they generally agree that a collection of people is a group when it evidences these qualities:

1. *Definable membership*: A collection of two or more people identifiable by name or type.
2. *Group consciousness*: The members think of themselves as a group. They have a "collective perception of unity," a conscious identification with each other.
3. *A sense of shared purpose*: The members have the same "object model," goals or ideals.
4. *Interdependence in satisfaction of needs*: The members need one another's help to accomplish the purposes for which they joined the group.
5. *Interaction*: The members communicate with one another, influence one another, and react to one another.
6. *Ability to act in a unitary manner*: The group can behave as a single organism.

SOURCE: Malcolm and Hulda Knowles, *Introduction to Group Dynamics* (Englewood Cliffs, NJ: Prentice Hall, 1972), pages 41-42.

## THE GROUP LEADER'S ROLE

*Guide*—Among the most important tasks a small-group leader assumes is to function as a guide for the group. This means the leader has a vision for what can happen in the group and leads the members in achieving that vision. The leader is not the boss or the spiritual giant, only the person who has the particular interest and training to help point the group in the chosen direction so every group member can share in a meaningful experience.

*Facilitator*—The group leader keeps the group moving. Setting the "tone," facilitating the conversation, stimulating caring, and assisting the decision-making process, the leader helps the group function well. The leader is responsible to keep the meetings organized and on track.

*Encourager*—The group leader sets the example for the group by encouraging the group members, looking after their special needs, and generally showing a spirit of caring. The leader is the chief encourager in the group.

*Prayer*—Praying for each group member, their individual and corporate concerns, is an important leadership task. The group leader must make a special effort to keep up with the group's prayer requests and pray for all the group members on a regular basis.

*Referee*—On occasion, a group member might present a problem that is too difficult for the person, the group, or the leader to effectively deal with. In this case, the leader must not hesitate to help the person find the needed assistance. Knowing the various referral resources is essential.

*Church Member*—The small-group leader must support the church's ministry wholeheartedly. A member and regular participant, the leader must strive always to view himself or herself as part of the leadership "we," not the impersonal "they." Group meetings are not the place to criticize one's church.

*Team Player*—The individual group leader is a vital member on the small-groups ministry team. He or she participates in this ministry with other leaders at various levels. Each group leader is expected to participate in corporate training and planning meetings. Furthermore, group leaders are encouraged to assist one another in whatever way possible.

Adapted from: Stephen R. Sheely, *Leader's Manual for Home Church Groups* (Austin, TX: Riverbend Baptist Church, n.d.).

## DISCIPLESHIP GROUP LEADER'S COMMITMENT

As we read Scripture, we cannot help but observe extremely high levels of commitment among God's leaders. So very often they encounter opposition, discouragement, even unresponsive people. Very likely, they made *a firm commitment in advance* that kept them from compromising when weary, discouraged, or upset. We are asking you to make that same *commitment in advance*.

The responsibilities expected of you as a discipleship group leader are listed here. Prayerfully make your commitment to God, and then let us know of your willingness to adhere to these guidelines.

1. I will seek to live a lifestyle that honors Christ and will not cause believers or unbelievers to stumble.
2. I will pray weekly for each person in my group.
3. I will thoroughly prepare my lesson each week.
4. I will lead the discipleship Bible study weekly.
5. I will be attentive to the spiritual, emotional, and physical needs of each individual in my group.
6. I will make every effort to telephone or write each person in my group at least once every two weeks to encourage him/her.
7. I will regularly attend Salem Alliance Church.
8. I will attend the leader's training retreat in September and the follow-up training meetings throughout the year. In case of an emergency, I will notify my discipleship coordinator and arrange for a substitute in my place. I recognize these meetings are essential to train and support me in:

   - Looking for opportunities to encourage each person in his or her personal walk with God and to lovingly urge each one to be a "doer of the Word and not a hearer only."
   - Being responsible to nurture the personal and spiritual growth of each individual in my group.
   - Creatively and effectively guiding the group discussion.
   - Handling difficult individuals and controversial questions.
   - Knitting the group together to care for and pray for one another.
   - Encouraging individuals to gain skills and enjoyment of studying God's Word on their own.

SOURCE: Salem Alliance Church (Salem, Oregon).

## RECRUITING INTERVIEW CHECKLIST

While it's not always a good idea to take this checklist with you when you interview a prospective small-group leader, be sure to do the following:

- ❑ Be warm and open. Help the person to feel comfortable.
- ❑ Quickly review why you are meeting (to discuss his or her potential involvement in the small-groups ministry).
- ❑ Explain the criteria used in selecting group leaders and why you feel he or she meets this criteria.
- ❑ Explain the small-groups ministry in general—the vision.
- ❑ Explain a group leader's role and responsibilities; provide a written job description.
- ❑ State the expected term of service.
- ❑ Inform the person who he or she can go to for assistance—the person's success is important to us.
- ❑ Show the person the available group materials and resources.
- ❑ Explain the training provided, including the opportunity (if available) to serve as an assistant leader, co-leader, etc., prior to leading a group.
- ❑ Allow the person the opportunity to ask questions and express feelings, fears, and needs.
- ❑ Reinforce the idea that this is a spiritual decision, that he or she has time to pray and consider the opportunity before you need an answer.
- ❑ Specify a definite amount of time before you'll contact the person for a decision. Arrange to answer any further questions that may arise.
- ❑ Thank the person for his or her time. Say that you are also praying for the person as he or she considers this important leadership position. Close with prayer.

SOURCE: Neal F. McBride, course materials from *Small Group Administration and Leadership Training*, Division of External and Continuing Education, Western Conservative Baptist Seminary, Portland, Oregon.

## TIPS ON INVOLVING MEMBERS TO ENHANCE GROUP OWNERSHIP

Divide the group tasks to relieve some of the group leader's duties and to help the group members develop a greater sense of "our group." Here are possibilities:

***Sharing Leader.*** One person leads the sharing time at the opening of each meeting by using the sharing questions provided in the study manual.

***Study Facilitator.*** A person assumes the responsibility to lead and/or make the necessary arrangements for someone to lead the study and/or discussion. This task is accomplished in cooperation with the wishes and desires expressed by all the group members.

***Prayer Captain.*** One group member maintains a prayer journal for the group and leads the group in praying for one another.

***Refreshments Coordinator.*** A member maintains a sign-up list and reminds group members when it is their turn to provide the refreshments.

***Social Coordinator.*** Someone plans and coordinates monthly social events.

***Child-Care Coordinator.*** One member makes the necessary arrangements for adequate child care.

Adapted from: Naegeli, Mary. *Handbook for Small Group Leaders*. (Menlo Park, CA: Menlo Park Presbyterian Church, 4th ed., 1990).

## SMALL GROUP COVENANT

Date:

Leader(s):

Members:


Unique goals of our group:


Curriculum we will study:


Attendance we expect:

How often we will meet:

When we will meet (day):

Our group is open these times:

Our group is limited to this number of people:

We will hold each other accountable by:


Hospitality:

Child Care:

Confidentiality:


Social Activities:

Other:


SOURCE: *Small Group Orientation* (Omaha, NE: Christ Community Church, n.d.).

## GROUP COVENANT

It's a good idea to set short-term goals and renew your covenant on a regular basis. Review this covenant with your group on the first night a new group meets, again after six or eight weeks, and then each time your group (1) begins a new unit of study, or (2) reconvenes after an extended period of absence (summer vacation, etc.).

*With God's help, for the next weeks, my covenant is to:*

- Make a commitment to the group, with attendance a priority.
- Give support and encouragement to the others in the group.
- Share stories of my "faith journey," including joys and struggles.
- Hold in confidence all that is shared in this group.
- Give permission to others to ask for spiritual help and prayer.
- Seek to grow in faith, life, love, and the mission of Jesus Christ.

*The specifics of our meetings will be:*

Weekly or bi-weekly:

Regular day of meeting:

Chosen time of meeting:

Place of meeting:

*Ground rules* (discuss and agree what to do about the following):

Refreshments:

Newcomers:

Absence:

Babysitting:

I will try with God's help to be a regular, faithful, caring member of this group.

Signed:

After your group makes its covenant, tell each group member to keep a copy in his or her Bible or study guide to refer to as a reminder of the promise to the group. At the end of your group's covenant period, conduct a time of evaluation when the members can discuss how they feel the group has done in view of the original goals; talk about ways to improve the overall experience. Ask if all group members wish to continue. Decide together if new people should be added. Consider options for your next study.

SOURCE: Mary Naegeli, *Handbook for Small Group Leaders* (Menlo Park, CA: Menlo Park Presbyterian Church, 4th edition, 1990).

## EXPANDING YOUR PROGRAM: REFINE PUBLICITY AND REGISTRATION PROCEDURES

The following recommendations are based on these three principles:

- The key to getting the church membership involved is the enthusiasm and encouragement provided by the senior pastor.
- A lot of publicity for a short period of time reaps the best results.
- The more people you can register at one time, the better you can appropriately group them according to their desires and needs.

*Enlist the senior pastor's help in promoting the small-group program.*

Several times a year our senior pastor chooses as the theme for his sermons our need to be in community to effectively live the Christian life. Some of his topics have been: "Why we need each other"; and "God never intended for His children to carry their burdens alone." He usually mentions specifically his belief that small groups are the best place to experience closeness, support, and care as members of the Body of Christ.

At other times of the year he will frequently mention registration time. He promotes our sign-ups during opening announcements from the pulpit. He often speaks to our new members classes and stresses that if new members have not formed at least a few close relationships within the first six months, they will most likely leave the church. He adds that joining a small group is the best way to form these close relationships, and he encourages every new member to sign up.

The support of other pastors for the program is extremely important as well. All our pastoral staff are instrumental in promoting participation.

*Publicize your small groups program in as many ways as possible only two or three times per year. Hold registration at these times and for no more than two or three weeks each time.*

We have found that when people think they can sign up anytime, they never get around to it. Their procrastination leads to apathy. By having only two registration times a year, with lots of publicity to promote it, we get a large number of people to register. During those same weeks, we also contact our present group leaders to see if they would like to add more people to their groups. It is then a relatively easy job to put new people into those groups with spaces available, or to start new groups which meet some or all the criteria the registrants desire. For most areas, we can group according to town or even neighborhood if we get a large registration.

Adapted from: Carla Bjorki, *Building a Small Groups Program from the Ground Up* (Menlo Park, CA: Menlo Park Presbyterian Church, 1990).

## THE FOUR BASIC PRINCIPLES OF ONE CHURCH'S CARE GROUP MINISTRY

A. Care Groups are one of the primary means of nurture and outreach in the life of Sunset Church.

B. Care Group Leaders are to assume pastoral oversight of members of their group. They will consider it their responsibility to provide pastoral care to the best of their ability when members of their group are in need.

C. The Care Groups will be open at all times to new people. All members of the group are free to bring guests, extended family members, or fellow church members to any of their meetings. Groups are challenged to grow and birth new groups at least annually.

D. Care Group Leaders and Assistant Leaders are expected to meet once each month with Pastors Ron and Ken, as well as their Overseers, for vision, accountability, and skill-training. At these meetings Pastor Ron will communicate primary events and decisions in the life and direction of the church that leaders can in turn communicate to their group members. Care Groups will become one of the primary means of communication at Sunset Church.

SOURCE: *The Care Group Leadership Training Manual* (Portland, OR: Sunset Presbyterian Church, 1990).

## WHAT ACCOMPLISHMENTS CAN SMALL GROUPS ACHIEVE?

Small groups are an excellent way to accomplish at least three necessary experiences that are vital to the life of a church committed to the biblical model. The activities of the small-group ministry at this church should contribute to the achievement of the following objectives:

*Objective One: Develop the spiritual maturity and personal worship of each group member.*

1. By providing an environment conducive to the study, discussion, and application of Scripture.
2. By encouraging members to pray for one another both during the meeting and throughout the week.
3. By providing a context for modeling and learning from the insight and experiences of others.
4. By providing meaningful opportunities for worship, praise, and singing.
5. By compelling group members to deal responsibly with spiritual issues on a regular basis.

*Objective Two: Promote fellowship among group members.*

1. By providing an environment in which group members can closely relate and openly communicate with each other.
2. By providing a context for sharing the common identity and experiences the group members have in Christ.
3. By providing specific opportunities wherein the group members must practice the "one another" commands in Scripture.
4. By encouraging a spirit of cooperation, commitment, and concern among group members.

*Objective Three: Stimulate ministry within and outside the church.*

1. By providing a context in which group members can discover and utilize their spiritual gifts.
2. By providing meaningful opportunities for group members to counsel and comfort those experiencing personal problems and pain.
3. By enabling and encouraging group members to share their faith with nonChristians.
4. By involving group members in the practice of good works within their church and community.

SOURCE: James D. Leake, *Facilitating Fellowship: A Training Manual For Small Group Leaders* (Venice, FL: Venice Bible Church, n.d.).

## EXAMPLES OF SUPPORT/RECOVERY GROUPS (Specialty Path Groups; see Step 4)

The Community Church of Joy in Glendale, Arizona, uses the specialty path groups listed here and others. In addition to this information, the publicity flyer lists time, location, and the person to call for more information.

*CARING FOR AGING PARENTS:* Few people are prepared for the responsibility and task involved in caring for older people.

*3D—DIET, DISCIPLINE, & DISCIPLESHIP:* This group includes a diet program, Bible study, tips on discipline, and sharing time.

*CODA* (Codependents Anonymous): Helps with recovery from codependence.

*HEALING THE HURTS OF THE PAST:* Group to support and help those who are victims of sexual or childhood abuse.

*ALCOHOLICS FOR CHRIST:* Twelve-Step weekly Bible study and support group designed for substance abusers and their families.

*GROWING BEYOND DIVORCE:* Focuses on the recovery process after divorce.

*G.L.A.D.* (Gallant Living After Death): For people who have suffered the loss of a loved one through death.

*SEXUAL ADDICTIONS SUPPORT:* Talking about problems and solutions.

*I.S.A.* (Incest Survivors Anonymous): A fellowship of men, women, boys, and girls who share their experiences, strengths, and hope for recovery.

*EMPTY NESTERS:* Children growing up and moving out? Come and discover the rest of God's plan for our lives.

*DOMESTIC VIOLENCE RECOVERY:* Focuses on the issues of abuse in the home.

*RAPE VICTIM SURVIVOR GROUP:* (No comment or explanation provided.)

*PARENTS OF HOMOSEXUALS/AIDS:* Support group for the parents of homosexuals and parents of those suffering from AIDS.

*HOMEMAKERS UNLIMITED:* Meets in a private home; mothers of young children discuss, learn, and laugh about daily concerns.

Rolling Hills Covenant Church in Portland, Oregon, uses these specialty path groups listed here.

*COPE AND HOPE:* Encouragement for women whose marriages are in crisis to apply the person and presence of God to their lives.

*FRIENDS IN RECOVERY:* A Christian support group for people recovering from the past effects of growing up in alcoholic and dysfunctional families. Our purpose is to help members in our fellowship overcome emotional pain and hurt from our families of origin and to be able to see their past in a new light.

*ANXIETY SUPPORT:* Learn to deal with phobias and anxieties. This group is for anyone who knowingly experiences anxiety episodes. We encourage each other.

*UNEQUALLY YOKED:* For married women who are spiritually single. Offers encouragement and mutual strength in a supportive context.

*WIDOWS' MIGHT:* A support group to rally around women who are newly widowed, as well as a friendship group for all widows.

*PARENTS OF CHILDREN WITH SPECIAL NEEDS:* For parents of children with physical, mental, emotional, or health issues. Provides resources, ideas, and encouragement.

THE BASIC DIFFERENCES BETWEEN COVENANT AND GROWTH GROUPS AT ONE CHURCH

## COVENANT GROUPS

Size: 10-14, males and females

Meet: Weekly for two hours in the evening

Commitment Level: Attendance and some preparation

Primary Elements: Singing, Bible study, sharing of needs, prayer

Leadership: Assigned couple or single who takes the primary leadership (others assist)

Also called: Traditional Bible study/support groups

## GROWTH GROUPS

Size: 4-6, same gender only

Meet: 1 to 1½ hours in the morning, at lunch, or in the evening

Commitment Level: All commit to read same daily devotional, weekly meeting, and open to discuss what you have read

Primary Elements: Talk about daily devotional reading and prayer

Leadership: One facilitator, but shared leadership

Also called: Accountability group

SOURCE: Paul R. Ford, Director of Discipleship, Heights Cumberland Presbyterian Church, Albuquerque, New Mexico.

## EVALUATING YOUR SMALL GROUP

1. As I see it, our purpose and goal(s) as a group was to . . .


2. In my opinion, we achieved our goal(s) . . .

   ❏ Completely  ❏ Almost completely  ❏ Somewhat  ❏ We blew it

3. We covenanted together at the beginning of this group. Did we keep our covenant?

   ❏ Yes  ❏ No  ❏ I cannot really say

4. In general, I found the group meetings (check all that apply) . . .

   ❏ Very helpful, relevant to my life  ❏ Intellectually stimulating
   ❏ Spiritually challenging  ❏ Life-changing  ❏ So-so  ❏ Often a waste of time
   ❏ Other (please specify):

5. In my opinion, overall our group functioned . . .

   ❏ Very well  ❏ Pretty good  ❏ Okay  ❏ Not too good  ❏ Terrible

6. I felt accepted by the other group members.

   ❏ Strongly agree  ❏ Agree  ❏ Somewhat agree  ❏ Somewhat disagree
   ❏ Disagree  ❏ Strongly disagree

7. Overall, the one thing I appreciated most about my group was . . .


8. The one thing I think the group could have done better was . . .


9. I recommend the following changes to our group covenant:



10. This group has stimulated my interest to remain in a similar small group.

    ❏ Strongly agree  ❏ Agree  ❏ Somewhat agree  ❏ Somewhat disagree
    ❏ Disagree  ❏ Strongly disagree  ❏ I don't know, perhaps another kind of group

11. In general, I think our church should . . .

    ❏ Increase its emphasis on small groups  ❏ Retain its present emphasis on small
    groups  ❏ Decrease its emphasis on small groups  ❏ Other (please specify):

## MAKING NEEDED ADJUSTMENTS BASED ON GROUP EVALUATION

Adjustments with your group or groups ministry are necessary at various times. However, all *programmatic and personnel modifications* must be done in a manner that . . .

- Results from careful evaluation
- Is based on shared reasoning; there is agreement among those involved
- Seeks the welfare of the involved individuals, while maintaining the groups ministry's integrity

The need to resolve many *procedural and/or administrative obstructions* is inevitable. Remember:

- People come before programs
- Change is not admitting failure
- There are many ways to accomplish a task
- Be systematic and complete
- Keep people informed

Evaluation includes recognizing and *giving appropriate recognition to individuals*.

*When?*
- Spiritual victories
- Lengthy service
- Job well done
- Personal accomplishment
- Team participation

*How?*
- Verbal praise
- "Honor roll"
- Public recognition
- Card or note
- Small memento (plaque, pin, etc).

Effective evaluation requires *establishing new and/or reaffirming existing goals and objectives*. Remember, goals and objectives . . .

- Provide direction (road map)
- Can and do change
- Must be realistic
- Must be shared and owned by everyone

Formal evaluation must never end; *initiate a new evaluation phase when a former one is complete*.

- Build an evaluation mind-set and routine
- Schedule evaluation as a regular occurrence

## ORGANIZATION OF HOME CHURCH GROUPS AT ONE CHURCH

***Supervision***: The pastor will oversee the operation of the small groups in the church. The home church group coordinator will report directly to the pastor. It is the task of the pastor to encourage the church to get involved in a group and to pass on to the coordinator which topics and issues the home groups should emphasize.

***Coordinator***: The coordinator has several important responsibilities, but the main task is to serve as an overseer of the different home church groups. The coordinator works with the pastor and the staff in order to provide leadership for the groups. The coordinator also works closely with the group leaders in order to assist them as they lead the different groups. The coordinator is also responsible for publicizing the home church group program to the church as a whole.

***Group Leaders***: Home church group leaders will undergo careful screening and comprehensive training before the groups actually begin to meet. The leader will function more as a facilitator for the group than as the one in charge.

***Meetings***: Home church group meetings will be weekly, on a day determined by the schedules of the different group members. Groups will be composed of the leaders and their families, associate leaders and their families, and the host family if different. Other church members and their families will also be assigned to the groups.

***Format of Meetings***: The order of a meeting will be determined by the needs and preferences of the group. This process will come under advisement of the leader, who will lead discussion on the purpose of the group and explain the different options for the group. Prayer, Bible study, testimonies, praise, confession, and discussion on certain issues (such as evangelism, church business, etc.) are some of these possibilities. The leader will guard against the possibility of a group becoming one-sided.

SOURCE: Stephen R. Sheely, *Leader's Manual for Home Church Groups* (Austin, TX: Riverbend Baptist Church, n.d.).

## AGENDA FOR A CARING GROUP LEADERS' MEETING AT ONE CHURCH—S.T.P.

### SHARING
- What are you doing to promote regular attendance?
- What information or resources can the church provide to help you?

### TIPS
- Evaluation is an important part of a growing ministry. The intent is to identify things that are going well and continue to do them and to identify areas of needed improvement and take the necessary steps to rectify the situation.
- Many people see evaluation as a "fault-finding" activity. It is important to present the idea to your group as an opportunity for growth and development as individuals and as a group.
- Constructive evaluation requires the following:
    1. Set aside a specific time to evaluate; during a regularly scheduled meeting. This is a decision you should make with your whole group.
    2. Stress the need for honesty. The normal tendency is to be either too polite, not wanting to hurt anyone's feelings, or too harsh, finding fault with everyone and everything. Caution against these extremes.
    3. Depending on your group's level of trust, you can seek their assessment by: (a) a group discussion where everyone verbally shares opinions of the group's progress or (b) written responses. Group members can first complete a questionnaire, then you read the responses without revealing who wrote them, and the group discusses the comments.
    4. Help your group examine these three areas (more are possible):
        a. *Format*: What you do and how you do what you do.
        b. *Relationships*: How you treat and respond to one another.
        c. *Details*: How often you meet, the place(s) where you meet, and the day and time you meet.
    5. Ask basic questions about each of the previous three fundamental areas:
        a. What do you like or appreciate about this area?
        b. What improvements do you think need to be made in this area?
    6. Identifying areas of positive results in your group up to this point is very important and should be the first thing you discuss. Help the group to explore how you can continue to do those things you are now doing well.
    7. Remember to remain positive when you begin to explore areas that need improvement. A negative attitude will spread like cancer. Spend as little time as possible identifying the trouble spots. The bulk of the time should be spent on remedies and specific plans for improvement.
- This whole process of evaluation should involve prayer before, during, and after your meeting.

### PRAYER
- What can we give praise for?
- What are areas of difficulty that need our prayers?

SOURCE: Montavilla Baptist Church, Portland, Oregon.

## THE HOLY SPIRIT AND SMALL GROUPS

The dynamics within small groups in the local church are similar to those in groups in other contexts, because groups involve people. However, unlike groups in other settings, when Christians meet together *the Holy Spirit is an unseen but real group member*.

Millard Erickson ("The Holy Spirit," *Christian Theology*, Grand Rapids, MI: Baker, 1986) suggests several implications from the doctrine of the Holy Spirit. With small groups in mind, four of his suggestions are worth special note:

1. The Holy Spirit is a person, not a vague force. Thus, He is someone with whom we can have a personal relationship, someone to whom we can and should pray.

2. The Holy Spirit empowers believers in their Christian life and service. Personal inadequacies should not deter or discourage us.

3. We may rely upon the Holy Spirit to give us understanding of the Word of God, and to guide us into His will for us.

4. It is appropriate to direct prayer to the Holy Spirit, just as to the Father and the Son. In such prayers we will thank Him for, and especially ask Him to continue, the unique work that He does in us.

As a member of the small group, the Holy Spirit influences the group's:

- Identity
- Purpose
- Members
- Atmosphere
- Leadership
- Direction
- Outcome

Like individual Christians, a small group can:

- *Give reverence* to the Holy Spirit
- *Obey* the Holy Spirit
- *Resist* the Holy Spirit
- *Grieve* the Holy Spirit

SOURCE: Neal F. McBride, course material in *Small Group Dynamics*, Division of External and Continuing Education, Western Conservative Baptist Seminary, Portland, Oregon.

SEVEN SIGNS OF SUCCESSFUL SMALL GROUPS

## 1. *Biblical Philosophy and Goals—A Vision*

- Clearly articulated what and why
- Shared (pastor and people know and understand the vision)

## 2. *Pastoral Support and Participation*

- Active leadership and participation by pastor(s)
- Pastor(s) sets the pace

## 3. *Integral to Church Life*

- More than an option—an expectation
- "Equal billing"
- People understand how groups fit into the church life
- Everyone participates? No . . . but 50% or more is ideal

## 4. *Equipped Leadership*

- The church takes seriously Ephesians 4:12
- Appointed . . . Prepared . . . Supported

## 5. *Flexible Structures—People Before Programs*

- Meets various needs for type of group and availability (day, time, etc.)
- People's needs are more important than programmatic needs
- Various group applications, formats, and agendas

## 6. *Purposeful/Effective Group Meetings*

- Well planned and conducted
- Meaningful relationships
- Life-related activities/content
- A wise stewardship of people's time

## 7. *Spiritual and Numerical Growth* (a sign shared with other programs offered by the church)

- More groups means more people and vice versa
- Evidence of both spiritual and numerical growth
- Demonstrated effectiveness

## OBJECTIONS TO SMALL GROUPS—Dealing with the Scary Questions

In developing a small-groups ministry, you are wise to identify and answer all the objections before someone else brings up the issues. Here are questions you must be ready to deal with:

1. Aren't small groups really just cliques?

2. Why do we have to change?

3. Will I be forced to participate?

4. Will I be in the same small group forever?

5. What if I don't like the other group members?

6. What if I don't like what the group does?

7. I tried once, it didn't work! Why try again?

8. I'm too busy! Where will I find the time?

9. Why isn't a group available when I'm available?

10. I don't like small groups! (I'm uncomfortable in small groups).

11. Is it okay to be nervous about being in a small group?

12. Do I have to?

13. Don't small groups cause church splits?

14. Can I come only when I feel like it?

15. Almost never heard any more: Small groups aren't biblical. But be prepared to answer this objection should it arise.

16. Et cetera. What questions may arise in your context and situation?

# AUTHOR

Neal F. McBride (Ed.D, Indiana University; Ph.D., Oregon State University) is president of Grace University (formerly, Grace College of the Bible) in Omaha, Nebraska. Dr. McBride's background includes serving as a seminary professor, professor of psychology, minister of education, youth pastor, church planter, and Air National Guard chaplain. He has worked with small groups of all kinds since 1969.